DEMOCRATIC
SCHOOLS

DEMOCRATIC SCHOOLS

Lessons from the chalk face

Edited by
MICHAEL W. APPLE AND
JAMES A. BEANE

OPEN UNIVERSITY PRESS
Buckingham

Open University Press
Celtic Court
22 Ballmoor
Buckingham
MK18 1XW

email: enquiries@openup.co.uk
world wide web: http://www.openup.co.uk

First published 1999

A catalogue record of this book is available from the British
Library

ISBN 0 335 20387 6 (pbk)

Typeset by Graphicraft Limited, Hong Kong
Printed in Great Britain by St Edmundsbury Press,
Bury St Edmunds, Suffolk

Contents

Notes on the contributors   vi

Acknowledgements   viii

Introduction   ix

1 The case for democratic schools   1
   James A. Beane and Michael W. Apple

2 Central Park East Secondary School:
   The hard part is making it happen   30
   Deborah Meier and Paul Schwarz

3 Beyond the shop: Reinventing vocational education   48
   Larry Rosenstock and Adria Steinberg

4 La Escuela Fratney: A journey towards democracy   68
   Bob Peterson

5 The situation made us special   98
   Barbara L. Brodhagen

6 Lessons from democratic schools   118
   Michael W. Apple and James A. Beane

Notes on the contributors

MICHAEL W. APPLE is John Bascom Professor of Curriculum and Instruction and Educational Policy Studies, University of Wisconsin, 225 N Mills Street, Madison, WI 53706, USA.

JAMES A. BEANE is Professor in the National College of Education, National-Louis University, Evanston, Illinois. Address correspondence to Dr Beane at 928 West Shore Drive, Madison, WI 53715, USA.

BARBARA L. BRODHAGEN teaches for the Madison Metropolitan Public Schools in Madison, Wisconsin. She can be reached at 928 West Shore Drive, Madison, WI 53715, USA.

DEBORAH MEIER is Co-Director of Central Park East Secondary School, 1573 Madison Avenue, New York, NY 10029, USA.

BOB PETERSON teaches 5th grade children at La Escuela Fratney in Milwaukee, Wisconsin. He is an editor of *Rethinking Schools*, which is available from Rethinking Schools Ltd, 1001 E Keefe Avenue, Milwaukee, WI 53212, USA. Tel: (414) 964–9646.

LARRY ROSENSTOCK is Executive Director of the Rindge School of Technical Arts, 459 Broadway, Cambridge, MA 02138, USA and is a Lecturer at the Harvard Graduate School of Education.

PAUL SCHWARZ is Co-Director of Central Park East Secondary School, 1573 Madison Avenue, New York, NY 10029, USA and is a Lecturer at the Harvard Graduate School of Education.

ADRIA STEINBERG is Academic Coordinator of the Rindge School of Technical Arts, 459 Broadway, Cambridge, MA 02138, USA.

Acknowledgements

The authors of this book wish to thank the thousands upon thousands of dedicated educators in schools throughout the world who daily demonstrate through their hard work and commitment what an education that is both critical and democratic can look like.

MICHAEL W. APPLE AND JAMES A. BEANE

Introduction: Lessons from the chalk face

Recently, one of us (Michael) was living in London for a period of time. He came upon a headline in one of the afternoon papers that read, if we may paraphrase, 'Radical Teachers Block Reforms'. Needless to say, he picked up a copy of the newspaper and read the story. It related how a group of primary school teachers were deeply upset with a new 'reform' policy that called for the restoration of 'setting' in their schools. They believed that such a policy was imposed without enough discussion and they were convinced that it would lead inexorably to even more sorting and selecting of students based on race and class. As he read the paper, one thing was very clear. While people in the USA and UK sometimes joked about 'being divided by the same language', the kinds of criticisms of schools and the kinds of 'reforms' being proposed to 'solve' these problems were strikingly similar. It was as if he was reading a paper from New York, or Chicago, or Los Angeles. Both sets of newspapers would undoubtedly say similar things: our nation and our economy need to be more competitive; schools are failing both the nation and its students; we need to return to what worked before, especially to 'real' knowledge and real discipline; teachers are blocking necessary changes. Both would claim that answers can be found in that odd combination of centralized control and market discipline. That these criticisms are not limited to the USA and the UK would be apparent to anyone who reads similar stories in the media in Australia and New Zealand as well.

The news report caused him to think even more about what was wrong with these kinds of stories. There *were* things that did indeed need to be changed in schools; but these new 'reform' policies seemed to be nearly guaranteed to make things worse rather than better. On returning to the United States, both of the editors of this book got together to discuss this issue. It soon became crystal clear that every instance we could think of where schools had been successful in actually dealing with the realities they faced went in the opposite direction. The book you are about to read shows why.

Democratic Schools tells the stories of four schools that have successfully put in place democratic and critical educational practices as guides to their entire curriculum. The schools are committed to an education that builds upon student and community needs, cultures, and histories. They are committed as well to anti-racist, anti-homophobic and anti-sexist principles, and are organized around a deep concern for social justice. These are not merely abstract principles, but are woven into the curriculum and teaching practices of the schools. The practices themselves involve a negotiated curriculum, extensive community and student involvement, and flexible forms of assessment. These are elementary, middle, and secondary schools that are all 'public' (that is, state supported), not private.[1] They are not 'ideal' schools, but 'real' schools in urban settings. All have significant concentrations of children of colour and economically poor children. In addition, all of them are faced with the very real challenges of limited budgets, insufficient human resources, the weight of bureaucratic rules, escalating demands for 'higher standards' and 'excellence', and so on. Yet each of these schools has succeeded in creating a challenging environment that is both serious academically and socially critical at the same time.

Accounts of each of these schools are told in the words of the educators who actually have put them into practice. The stories are told honestly, without omitting the tensions and struggles that have gone with the very evident successes. This is crucial, since the literature in education is filled with overly romantic portrayals of easy victories in the struggle to reform our schools. Yet, there are no easy victories. Each site required risks and overcoming bureaucratic and ideological challenges. However, even with these tensions and challenges, these schools provide evidence that even in a time of movement back to conservative ideologies of education and serious fiscal problems, it is possible to build and defend critical educational policies and practices in real schools in ways that benefit students, teachers, and local communities. These victories happened in areas that are currently among the most contentious: making connections between schooling and the world of work, connecting the school curriculum to the multiple cultures of ethnically diverse students and communities, creating models of content and pedagogy that even alienated students find personally meaningful, creating conditions that involve communities deeply in the education of their children, and making the classroom and the school places where teachers themselves find their work fulfilling and satisfying.

The educators who tell their stories here – at least officially – do not have to deal with some of the constraints that teachers, heads, parents, and community members have to confront in the UK. After all, there is no Ofsted in the USA. There is no official national curriculum and there is no officially recognized national testing programme that is linked to a national curriculum. Further, the intense demand to engage in the marketization of education is just taking off in the USA, in part stimulated by overly positive portrayals of what supposedly has happened in England and Wales.[2] Think of it: no 'league tables'; no prespecified national curriculum or national testing programme; somewhat fewer worries about image in the face of a competitive school market.

Yet this totally romanticizes the situation that these educators face, for the differences are minor compared with the overwhelming similarities. While there is no national curriculum in the United States, there is a *de facto* national curriculum. This is established by textbooks in every subject, textbooks that are written to very tight and very specific government directed content guidelines in the most powerful states. Publishers simply will not publish anything that is not likely to be approved and purchased in populous states, such as Texas and California. Thus, in a nation where the curriculum tends to be the standardized textbooks, the entire nation basically teaches what sells in a very limited number of states. Because of this, there is clearly a national curriculum. It is just more hidden from view.[3]

This is made even more powerful because of the ways in which the media work. There is a constant barrage of news reports about failing schools. Such reports call for a 'return' to 'traditional' subjects and traditional models of teaching. Thus, teachers are under unremitting pressure to teach what well-organized and well-funded (and usually conservative) groups have decided are appropriate content and methods.

Further, the vast majority of states now have programmes of state-wide testing in all of the major subject areas. Increasingly, teachers are having to 'teach for the tests'. Even if they want to maintain their autonomy on this, most of the content and textbooks that are officially seen to be necessary are closely interconnected to the mandated tests in many cities and states. In essence, the 'tail of the test wags the body of the curriculum'. Unfortunately, American schools are more and more dominated by ideas that seem to rest on the belief that if it moves in the classroom, it must be measured, and if it has not moved yet, measure it in case it does move tomorrow. We do not want to be overly 'cute' here, but the situations that teachers and other educators face in the UK and the USA are really much more similar than what one might assume at first glance, especially since the results of these test scores are widely published in newspapers and are used to compare schools.

To take another example, all of this is connected with increasingly specified and reductive lists of goals, content to be covered and values to be taught. While this is not determined at a national level as in England and Wales, states and cities throughout the country are developing such lists and are increasingly holding teachers and administrators strictly accountable to them. 'Standard attainment targets', more often called 'standards and benchmarks' in the USA, are certainly not invisible to say the least. While there is nothing necessarily wrong with systems of accountability, many of these are imposed, are inflexible and are put in place with little thought about what is actually happening in classrooms given the growth of poverty, the effects of joblessness, the destruction of social safety nets, the decline of inner cities and so on. Thus, these too often serve as excuses for powerful groups to blame hard working educators for things over which they have little control.

Yet it is not only the existence of such standardized targets that needs to be focused upon. Often the specific contents of these standards are imposed from above. Perhaps an example may be helpful here. In our own state, Wisconsin, the Department of Public Instruction (the state's equivalent of a ministry of education) spent a number of years developing standards from the ground up. Teachers, administrators, academics, community members, activists, and others were deeply involved in developing them, in rewriting them to make them more flexible and more responsive and useful, and in discussions over their implementation. The conservative governor of the state, in concert with a large bloc of legislators who often talk about 'decentralization' but in fact are just as deeply committed to centralizing control over curricula, teaching, and evaluation, called for their rejection and had them radically rewritten to conform to the content guidelines established by a nationally powerful rightist 'think-tank'. The new standards do not look much like those more democratically arrived at ones that were nearing completion earlier.

This clearly connects to another similarity that educators on both sides of the Atlantic are facing. As in England and Wales, all of the teachers represented in *Democratic Schools*, have had to deal with the heavy hand of bureaucratic authority. Managerialism – where demands for ever more efficiency, cost-cutting and ever higher test scores seem to escalate – is linked to equally strong demands to connect the school to the 'needs' of the economy. Competitiveness, standards, excellence, the 'basics' – these are the watchwords. Anything else is simply a luxury we supposedly cannot afford.

The effects of all of this on schools throughout the country have been predictable. There has been an increase in teachers' stress, an intensification of teachers' work, a redefinition of administrators' roles into caring less and less about the actual substance of curricula and teaching and more and more about a school's image, and a definite feeling (one that we believe is based on an accurate perception) that educators and local communities have actually lost autonomy and control rather than having gained them. Listening to educators speak in the USA echoes almost word for word the worries that are so visible in the UK as well. Administrators and teachers constantly worry on both sides of the Atlantic about being 'increasingly forced into a position in which they have to demonstrate performance along centralised curricula in a context where they have diminishing control'.[4] In both contexts, then, teachers and heads (principals, as they are called in the United States) experience considerably heavier work loads and ever escalating demands for accountability, a seemingly never ending schedule of meetings, and in very many cases a growing scarcity of resources both emotional and material.[5] Deskilling and demoralization are not the paths to democratic and critical education, but are the very opposite.

Other similarities are also striking. On both sides of the Atlantic pressure to 'marketize' schooling seems to have similar effects. Despite the claims that 'marketization' will create alternatives, the market does not seem to encourage diversity in curriculum, pedagogy, organization, clientele, or even image. It consistently seems to devalue alternatives and consistently increases the power of traditional models of teaching and learning. This return to 'tradition' has had some rather unsurprising results, unfortunately. More critical models of curriculum and teaching are delegitimated. Restratification, through tracking, streaming, and setting, is reintroduced and the possibility of detracking is made even less probable. More emphasis is given to 'gifted' children and 'fast track' classes, while students who are seen as less academically able are therefore 'less attractive'. That all this exacerbates differences in access and outcome based on class, race and gender should come as no surprise.[6] Thus, although there may be differences in where formal authority rests and in where control comes from, this should not lead us to assume that teachers on both sides of the Atlantic – and in Australia, New Zealand, and elsewhere – are facing totally dissimilar situations. Unfortunately, they clearly are not.

Many of these policies and practices came about because of the ability of powerful neoliberal and neoconservative groups to blame educators for unemployment, a supposed loss of traditional knowledge and values, and just about everything that was wrong with society. Their proposed solution was nearly the same in both places – gain more control, put in place detailed 'high stakes' tests, hold teachers and principals strictly accountable for results, and so on. At the same time, there was a push for marketization so that not only the government but parents seeking a competitive edge for their children would put pressure on schools to respond to market demands, no matter what the cost to social justice both to identifiable groups of mainly poor students and to more democratic and critical educational practices that might actually better serve the needs of those students and communities that are now so ill-served by both existing curricula and the more traditional models being promoted by the market.

As one might expect, all of these pressures have made life difficult for educators. Yet, difficult does not mean impossible. As in the UK, this has stimulated a considerable amount of critical reflection on the part of teachers and administrators in the USA. Yet, also as in the UK, the reactions have not stopped at criticism. Educators have developed some very thoughtful and practical ways of organizing curricula, teaching and evaluation that – even in the face of standardized curricula, reductive and constant assessments, and demands to cut both costs and 'frills' – are successful in terms of meeting both external needs and their own deeply felt convictions about a responsive and socially just education.

The chapters included in *Democratic Schools* demonstrate what can happen when educators, parents, community activists, and students respond in creative ways to all of these pressures. They are eloquent reminders that education is not only preparation for life but life itself. We are certain that similar stories can be found in cities and towns throughout the UK. In fact, we have seen many of them in action in schools throughout Britain, Australia, New Zealand, and wherever we have travelled to work with and learn from educators who are making a real difference in the lives of their children and their communities. If the examples provided in this book stimulate other democratic educators to tell their own stories so that they can teach each other about what *really* works, this book will have more than served its purpose.

All of the authors involved in *Democratic Schools* have been truly heartened by the reception that has greeted the book. We felt all along both that the ways in which the major media portrayed teachers and other educators and that the blame that was heaped on them from conservative critics simply did not come close to capturing the amount of effort teachers were devoting to making a difference in young people's lives. In the media portrayals of educators as uncaring, uncreative, selfish (and overpaid and lazy) people who needed to be pushed by both market competition and centralized control over curriculum and testing now being so widely circulated, we certainly did not recognize the teachers and principals with whom we worked. We disagreed sharply with the increasingly widespread idea that all of the progressive educational policy and practices instituted earlier in our own country and elsewhere had been a failure. Instead, we were certain that there were large numbers of untold successes and that there were many, many teachers who were more than a little distressed by what they now were being asked to do and what they now were being asked *not* to do. We believed that one of the things that was needed was an accurate picture of what it *is* possible to do, even in this time of conservatism when even the major governing parties in the USA and in the UK seem to have accepted large portions of the conservative educational and social agenda.

While we knew that many other educators – especially 'at the chalk face', so to speak – felt very much the same way, little did we expect the response that this slim book has received. At last count, more than 250,000 copies are in the hands of educators in the United States. The Japanese Teachers Union has published their own edition of the book. Translations of it have become something of a rallying point for democratic educators in Brazil, Argentina, Chile, Spain and elsewhere as well. This tells us something of great importance, we believe. Educators, community activists, and progressive members of government in many nations are constantly looking for ways that enable them to put their most deeply felt democratic ideals into practice. Of course, no one book can ever give us the answers to all of our questions about what we can do to actually succeed. But our hope is that you will find some powerfully evocative answers to the question 'What do I do on Monday?' in the stories told by these practicing educators. All of them are fundamentally committed to restoring collective memory and to keeping the vast river of democracy on course in the schools, classrooms and communities in our nations. All of them, like so many of you in the UK, are now doing all that they can to make certain that the headlines found in that London newspaper, and the assumptions about what education should look like, are wrong.

Notes

1 While it may vary, the school system in the United States is largely organized around a three school model: elementary schools, which include kindergarten up to fifth or six grade (5-year-olds up to 11–12-year-olds); middle schools or junior high schools, which include grades six or seven to eight or nine (11–12-year-olds to 13–14-year-olds); and secondary or high schools, which include grades nine or ten up to twelve (13–14-year-olds up to 17–18-year-olds).

2 This is best seen in John Chubb and Terry Moe (1990) *Politics, Markets, and America's Schools*. Washington: Brookings Institution. Criticisms of such proposals are widespread, as you might imagine. See, for example, Michael W. Apple (1996) *Cultural*

Politics and Education. Buckingham: Open University Press and Alex Molnar (1996), *Giving Kids the Business.* Boulder: Westview Press.

3 See Michael W. Apple (1993) *Official Knowledge: Democratic Education in a Conservative Age.* London: Routledge and James A. Beane (1997), *Curriculum Integration: Designing the Core of Democratic Education.* New York: Teachers College Press.

4 Geoff Whitty, Sally Power, and David Halpin (1998) *Devolution and Choice in Education.* Buckingham: Open University Press, p. 63. This volume is a rich source of comparisons between the USA and England and Wales – one that includes data on New Zealand and Australia as well.

5 Ibid, pp. 67–68.

6 Ibid, pp. 119–120.

1

JAMES A. BEANE AND MICHAEL W. APPLE

The case for democratic schools

Pasadena, California, 1937. *A group of 3rd graders has spent several weeks studying problems in their school, homes, neighbourhoods, and community. Besides looking at problems they know of, they have also gathered examples from parents, teachers, and community officials. After a month of research and discussion, they collect their recommendations for solving these problems in a booklet that will be distributed throughout the community.*

Baltimore, Maryland, 1953. *The streets in one neighbourhood of this city are filled for a week by high-school students conducting a door-to-door voter registration drive among ethnic minority residents. This is but one of many projects they have worked on this year, including a civil defence survey, a community health campaign, and a study of housing relocation problems.*

Port Jarvis, New York State, 1972. *Though it is a cold, snowy night, nearly 125 students, teachers, administrators, parents, board members, and representatives of various community organizations are meeting to consider projects they might undertake to redesign their schools. Among others, they will make arrangements to distribute school newsletters in languages other than English, plan a new community youth centre, start a radio programme produced by students, set up mentorships for young people with adults in the community, and arrange to make the school more available for community activities.*

Ulysses, Pennsylvania, 1979. *Just as they do every Friday afternoon, the students and teachers in the elementary school gather today to discuss ongoing schoolwide projects and problems. The major issue this week is that someone has written graffiti on a school wall. After nearly a half-hour of debate, three proposals are put forth. The group votes to establish a new rule: anyone defacing school property will spend their free time over three days working with the school caretaker.*

Belvidere, Illinois, 1990. *Looking through a classroom window at the dust-cart below, a student asks the teacher, 'Where does that rubbish go?' Just as curious, the teacher arranges for a class field trip to an area landfill. Concerned about the size and contents of the landfill, the students undertake a campaign for conservation and recycling in their school. Over several months, their efforts begin to take hold. Although they are just 1st graders, they have made a difference in their school.*

Madison, Wisconsin, 1991. *On a warm September day, a group of nearly 60 middle-school students and their teachers are working together to create their curriculum out of questions and concerns they have about themselves and their world. Eventually they cluster their questions into themes such as 'Living in the Future', 'Problems in the Environment', 'Isms' and 'Conflict'. After selecting their first theme and planning relevant activities, they will spend the year trying to answer those questions – their questions.*

All of us have heard stories like these and know that while not rare, they are unusual. All took place in public schools. All involved real young people, real educators and real communities no different on the surface than thousands of others. Yet there is something about these stories, a sometimes elusive feeling, that appeals to a deep sense of what a worthwhile and valuable education ought to look like. What are these people working on? Who is involved? How are they working together? Who benefits from such work? If we think about these stories and questions, we may eventually begin to see what is really happening. Perhaps we will begin to remember a now half-forgotten idea that was to guide the purposes and programmes of our public schools. The idea was, and is, democracy.

In the midst of widespread attacks on education, we must keep alive the long tradition of democratic school reform that has played such a valuable role in making many schools lively and powerful places for those who go to them. Rather than giving up on the idea of the 'public' schools and moving down the path towards privatization, we need to focus on schools that work. Despite some people's relentless attempts to make us think otherwise, we do not have to resign ourselves to choosing between a failing public school system and market initiatives such as voucher plans or for-profit 'public' schools run by private firms, such as the Edison Project or Education Alternatives Inc in the USA. There are public schools throughout the USA where the hard work of teachers, administrators, parents, community activists, and students has paid off. These are the schools that are alive with excitement, even in sometimes depressing and difficult circumstances. These are the schools in which teachers and students alike are engaged in serious work that results in rich and vital learning experiences for all.

The idea of democratic schools has fallen on hard times, however. All around us, we can see the signs. Public schools are called on to educate all of our children, yet are simultaneously blamed for the social and economic disparities that severely detract from their chances of successfully doing so. Local decision making is glorified in political rhetoric at the same time that legislation is introduced to put in place national standards, a national curriculum, and national tests. Demands are made to emphasize critical thinking while censorship of school programmes and materials increases. Census figures display growing cultural diversity while pressure is applied to keep the curriculum within the narrow boundaries of the Western cultural tradition. The needs of business and industry are suddenly the pre-eminent goals of our educational system. Education in morality and ethics is reduced to a litany of behaviour traits. Privileged groups seek to flee comprehensive, diverse public schools through vouchers, tax credits, 'choice' plans and exclusionary programmes for their 'gifted' children. US federal officials pronounce the public schools a failure while effectively suppressing a report that shows these officials have misused their own statistics (Jensen 1994).

Could it be that the century-long struggle for democratic purposes and practices in education and schooling never occurred? How could our collective memory have failed so easily? *Thematic unit teaching* and *curriculum integration* have become buzz words in educational circles, but have we forgotten that both concepts have their roots in the problem-centred 'core' approaches advocated by earlier progressive social reconstructionists? How can we disconnect the call for heterogeneous grouping, advocated by so many groups today, from the longer struggle of the civil rights movement? Are 'developmentally appropriate' practices a recent invention, or do they stretch back to the progressive, child-centred schools created early in this century? When we speak of cooperative learning today, shall we simply ignore the cooperative group process work done in schools and communities as part of democratic movements since the 1920s? How can we seem puzzled by ways to connect schools to their communities when so many stories of significant service projects can be found in the professional literature of at least the past 60 years?

Rosa Parks is often portrayed during Black History Month as simply a 'tired, older woman' who wanted to sit down on a bus. But her courageous act on that bus came after months of work on resistance and civil disobedience at the Highlander Folk School.[1] Likewise, many of our most trusted and powerful ideas about schooling are the hard-won gains of long and courageous efforts to make our schools more democratic (see, for example, Rugg 1939). We are the beneficiaries of those efforts, and we have an obligation to carry forward the demanding dream of public schools for a democratic society.

The questions raised here are meant to remind us of that half-forgotten dream, to rouse us from the stupor we fell into nearly 20 years ago. Although our memories may have become blurred, we can still recall that public schools are essential to democracy. We cannot help but be jolted wide awake when discussions about what works in schools, what should be done in schools, make no mention of the role of public schools in expanding the democratic way of life. Hence, we must make the case again.

The meaning of democracy

Those of us who live in the United States of America claim that democracy is the central tenet of our social and political relations. It is, we say, the basis for how we govern ourselves, the concept by which we measure the wisdom and worth of social policies and shifts, the ethical anchor we seek when our political ship seems to drift. And it is the standard we use to measure the political progress of other countries as well as their trade status with our own.

It is not surprising, then, that the word 'democracy', seems to be heard more frequently these days. In many places around the world, oppressed peoples struggle for human and civil rights. Dictatorships and popularly elected governments are overthrown at a startling rate. In the United States of America, growing numbers of people claim that politicians at all levels are no longer in touch with their constituents. Conflict among political, religious, and cultural groups fuels debate over free speech, privacy, land use, lifestyles, and, throughout it all, the rights of the individual in relation to the interests of the larger society. Amid this dissonance, the idea of democracy presumably serves as a crucial benchmark for judging events and ideas.

Central tenets and ethical anchors, however, also tend to be converted into rhetorical slogans and political codes to gain popular support for all manner of ideas. Thus, they are fraught with ambiguity. 'Democracy' is no exception. Woodrow Wilson understood this well when he deflected opposition to US involvement in World War I with the virtually unassailable statement that our soldiers were fighting 'to make the world safe for democracy'. Calling forth the word 'democracy' did the trick then and has done so for a wide array of political and military manœuvres since.

The meaning of democracy is just as ambiguous in our own times, and the rhetorical convenience of that ambiguity is more evident than ever (Apple 1988). One can understand, for example, how claims for democracy could be used to shore up movements for civil rights, expanded voting privileges, and protection of free speech. Democracy is also used, however, to further the causes of free market economies and school-choice vouchers, and to defend the dominance of two major political parties. We hear the democracy defence used countless times every day to justify almost anything people want to do: 'Hey, we live in a democracy, right?'

On the other hand, it is not uncommon to hear some people say that democracy has simply become irrelevant, that it is too inefficient or dangerous in an increasingly complex world. For these people, the democracy defence itself has become cumbersome or, perhaps, not sufficient to get them what they want. In a society like that of the USA, where there are clear divisions of wealth and power, the freedoms and ambiguity associated with democracy have clearly benefited some people more than others. Efforts to sharpen the definition of democracy and extend its meaning throughout society are seen by some of the more privileged people of this country as threats to their own status and power. To understand this view, we need only look at the startling contradiction between the movement for greater school achievement on the one hand and the resistance to equitable spending for all schools on the other.

Under these complicated conditions, a book on democratic schools may seem almost foolhardy. After all, if the meaning of democracy is so confused in the larger society, how can we possibly settle on its meaning for everyday life in schools? That risk in mind, we have gone ahead, buoyed by certain beliefs. We believe that democracy does mean something and that bringing that meaning to light is critical at a time when many citizens are vigorously debating the future course of our schools. Moreover, we find it hard to imagine that people who have known the privileges of democracy would so easily give them up. We find it even harder to imagine that they would not want these privileges for their children, indeed for all people. We admit to having what Dewey and others have called the 'democratic faith', the fundamental belief that democracy has a powerful meaning, that it can work, and that it is necessary if we are to maintain freedom and human dignity in our social affairs.

Democracy works in multiple ways in social affairs. Most of us who attended school in the USA (and perhaps elsewhere) were taught that democracy is a form of political governance involving the consent of the governed and equality of opportunity. For example, we learned that citizens may directly and fully participate in such events as elections while being represented in other matters by those we elect to federal and state legislatures as well as boards and committees governing local school policy.

Less explicitly taught were the conditions on which a democracy depends, the foundations of 'the democratic way of life' (Beane 1990). It is these conditions and their extension through education that are the central concerns of democratic schools. Among such conditions are the following:

1 The open flow of ideas, regardless of their popularity, that enables people to be as fully informed as possible.
2 Faith in the individual and collective capacity of people to create possibilities for resolving problems.
3 The use of critical reflection and analysis to evaluate ideas, problems, and policies.
4 Concern for the welfare of others and 'the common good'.
5 Concern for the dignity and rights of individuals and minorities.
6 An understanding that democracy is not so much an 'ideal' to be pursued as an 'idealized' set of values that we must live and that must guide our life as a people.
7 The organization of social institutions to promote and extend the democratic way of life.

If people are to secure and maintain a democratic way of life, they must have opportunities to learn what that way of life means and how it might be led (Dewey 1916). Although common sense alone tells us this is a true statement, there is perhaps no more problematic concept in education than that of democratic schools, a concept that some consider almost an oxymoron. How can this be so? Simply put, many people believe that democracy is nothing more than a form of federal government and thus does not apply to schools and other social institutions. Many also believe that democracy is a right of adults, not of young people. And some believe that democracy simply cannot work in schools.

Others are committed to the idea that the democratic way of life is built upon opportunities to learn what it is about and how to lead it. They believe that the schools, as a common experience of virtually all young people, have a moral obligation to introduce them to the democratic way of life. They know, as well, that such a life is learned by experience. It is not a status to be attained only after other things are learned. Moreover, they believe that democracy extends to all people, including the young. Finally, they believe that democracy is neither cumbersome nor dangerous, that it can work in societies and it can work in schools. As Maxine Greene (1985, p. 4) writes, 'Surely it is an obligation of education in a democracy to empower the young to become members of the public, to participate, and play articulate roles in the public space.'

Those committed to creating democratic schools, however, also understand that doing so involves more than the education of the young. Democratic schools are meant to be democratic places, so the idea of democracy also extends to the many roles that adults play in the schools. This means that professional educators as well as parents, community activists, and other citizens have a right to fully informed and critical participation in creating school policies and programmes for themselves and young people.

Proponents of democratic schools also realize, sometimes painfully, that exercising democracy involves tensions and contradictions. Democratic participation in decision making, for example,

opens the way for antidemocratic ideas such as the continuing demands for censorship of materials, the use of public tax
vouchers for private school tuition, and the maintenance of
historical inequities in school life. Furthermore, there always
looms the possibility of the illusion of democracy, in which
authorities may invite participation so as to 'engineer consent'
for predetermined decisions (Graebner 1988). Such contradictions and tensions point to the fact that bringing democracy
to life is always a struggle. But beyond them lies the possibility
for professional educators and citizens to work together in
creating more democratic schools that serve the common good
of the whole community.

This book is for and about educators who are committed to
democracy, who value the democratic way of life, who believe
that schools can be democratic places, and who have the courage to carry those beliefs into action. In several chapters we
will hear some of these educators describe, in their own voices,
how they have brought the idea of democracy to life in their
schools and classrooms. These are remarkable stories inas-
much as the very idea of democratic schools has proved to be
so elusive to the educational community. The stories are not
filled with the easy promises and slick slogans of packaged
programmes or systems. Instead, like almost all school stories,
they reveal the hard work and commitment of real educators
struggling to create and maintain arrangements that reveal the
deeply held values that they, and we, believe must be acted on
now. The authors of this book are fundamentally dissatisfied
with the conservative solutions usually put at centre stage since
the 1970s: tighter centralized control, standardization of content, more reductive testing and so on. All of us believe that
we must move beyond handwringing and find real answers to
the question 'What works in schools?'

What is a democratic school?

Before presenting the real life stories in this book, we want to
offer a context for their telling. What is a democratic school?
What might we expect to see if we visited one? What are its

underlying principles? How has the concept of democratic schools emerged over time? What threatens the existence of these schools? How can it be that these stories are so remarkable in a society that purports to be democratic?

Democratic schools, like democracy itself, do not happen by chance. They result from explicit attempts by educators to put in place arrangements and opportunities that will bring democracy to life (see, for example, Bastian *et al.* 1986; Wood 1988, 1992). These arrangements and opportunities involve two lines of work. One is to create democratic structures and processes by which life in the school is carried out. The other is to create a curriculum that will give young people democratic experiences.

Democratic structures and processes

To say that democracy rests on the consent of the governed is almost a cliché, but in a democratic school it is true that all of those directly involved in the school, including young people, have the right to participate in the process of decision making. For this reason, democratic schools are marked by widespread participation in issues of governance and policy making. Committees, councils and other schoolwide decision-making groups include not only professional educators, but also young people, their parents and other members of the school community. In classrooms, young people and teachers engage in collaborative planning, reaching decisions that respond to the concerns, aspirations and interests of both. This kind of democratic planning, at both the school and the classroom levels, is not the 'engineering of consent' towards predetermined decisions that has too often created the illusion of democracy, but a genuine attempt to honour the right of people to participate in making decisions that affect their lives.

We must remember, however, that local decision making must still be guided by democratic values. It is one of the contradictions of democracy that local, populist politics do not always serve democratic ends. After all, left entirely to local discretion, we might still have schools characterized by legal racial segregation and denial of access to all but the wealthy.

In short, the realization of democratic schools does in part depend on selective intervention of the state, especially where the process and content of local decision making serve to disenfranchise and oppress selected groups of people. While such intervention is usually unpopular among those who have sought exclusive power, it serves as a reminder that the wide distribution of rights and other democratic values are meant to be more than principles on paper.

Our own times offer many illustrations of the tension between the state's obligation to safeguard democracy and the democratic right of interest groups to air their views. For example, public schools in a democratic society are meant to offer access to, and critical examination of, a wide range of ideas. Meanwhile, various special interest groups, especially religious fundamentalists, demand that ideas and materials open to consideration in schools be limited to those supporting their groups' own values (Delfattore 1993). At the same time, local groups across the political spectrum are troubled by moves to create a national curriculum in which the range of knowledge studied is limited to that deemed important by select groups at the national level. The idea of widespread participation in school affairs as a feature of democratic schools is thus not as simple as inviting participation, because the right to 'have a say' introduces questions about how various viewpoints fit into the fragile equation balancing special interests and the larger 'common good' of the democratic community.

Those involved in democratic schools see themselves as participants in communities of learning. By their very nature, these communities are diverse, and that diversity is prized, not viewed as a problem. Such communities include people who reflect differences in age, culture, ethnicity, gender, socio-economic class, aspirations and abilities. These differences enrich the community and the range of views it might consider. Separating people of any age on the basis of these differences or using labels to stereotype them simply creates divisions and status systems that detract from the democratic nature of the community and the dignity of the individuals against whom such practices work so harshly.

While the community prizes diversity, it also has a sense of shared purpose. No matter what the privatizers or those who want economic rationality to drive schools say, democracy is not simply a theory of self-interest that gives people license to pursue their own goals at the expense of others; the common good is a central feature of democracy. For this reason, the communities of learners in democratic schools are marked by an emphasis on cooperation and collaboration rather than competition. People see their stake in others, and arrangements are created that encourage young people to improve the life of the community by helping others.

In all these arrangements, and in the policy decisions that support them, people in democratic schools persistently emphasize structural equity. While initial access to educational opportunities is understood to be a necessary aspect of democratic schools, access alone is not considered sufficient for their realization. In an authentically democratic community, all young people are also considered to have the right of access to all programmes in the school and to the outcomes the school values. For this reason, those in democratic schools seek to assure that the school includes no institutional barriers to young people. Every effort is made to eliminate tracking, biased testing and other arrangements that so often deny such access on grounds of race, gender and socioeconomic class.

Educators who are committed to democracy realize that sources of inequity in the school are likely to be found in the community as well. At the very least, they understand that the possibilities arising from democratic experiences in the school may too easily be washed away by life on the outside (Gutmann 1987). In seeing themselves as part of the larger community, they seek to extend democracy there, not only for the young but for all people. In short, they want democracy on a large scale; the school is just one of the sites on which they focus. This is a crucial point. The educational landscape is littered with the remains of failed school reforms, many of which failed because of the social conditions surrounding the schools. Only those reforms that recognize these conditions and actively engage them are likely to make a lasting difference in the lives of the children, educators and communities served by the schools.

It is this last point in particular that distinguishes democratic schools from other kinds of 'progressive' schools, such as those that are simply humanistic or child-centred. Democratic schools are both of those in many ways, but their vision extends beyond purposes such as improving the school climate or enhancing students' self-esteem. Democratic educators seek not simply to lessen the harshness of social inequities in school, but to change the conditions that create them. For this reason, they tie their understanding of undemocratic practices inside the school to larger conditions on the outside. The case for heterogeneous grouping, for example, is made partly on grounds of increased academic and social achievement, but more broadly on grounds of justice and equitable access as profound social issues (Oakes 1985). Like other progressive educators, those involved with democracy care deeply about young people, but they also understand that such caring requires them to stand firm against racism, injustice, centralized power, poverty, and other gross inequities in school and society.

The initial sketch of the structures and processes essential to democratic schools can be done rather quickly, but the fully rendered picture is not so easily realized. The work involved in organizing and keeping alive a democratic school is exhausting and ripe with conflict. After all, despite the rhetoric of democracy in our society and the common-sense idea that the democratic way of life is learned through democratic experiences, schools have been remarkably undemocratic institutions. While democracy emphasizes cooperation among people, too many schools have fostered competition – for grades, for status, for resources, for programmes, and so on. While democracy depends on caring for the common good, too many schools, stimulated by the influence of political agendas imposed from outside, have emphasized an idea of individuality based almost entirely on self-interest. While democracy prizes diversity, too many schools have largely reflected the interests and aspirations of the most powerful groups in this country and ignored those of the less powerful. While schools in a democracy would

presumably demonstrate how to achieve equal opportunity
for all, too many schools are plagued by structures such as
tracking and ability grouping that deny equal opportunity and
results to many, particularly the poor, people of colour and
women.

Those who are committed to democratic education are often
placed in a position of conflict with the dominant traditions
of schooling. At almost every turn, their ideas and efforts
are likely to be resisted by both those who benefit from the
inequities of schools and those who are more interested in
efficiency and hierarchical power than in the difficult work
of transforming schools from the bottom up. The frustrations
involved in creating democratic schools are only exceeded by
the more ambitious task of maintaining them in the face of
non-democratic currents in public opinion and educational
policy. Democratic educators understand, however, that democracy does not present an 'ideal state' crisply defined and waiting to be attained. Rather, a more democratic experience is
built through their continual efforts at making a difference.
The undertaking is not an easy one; it is filled with contradictions, conflict, and controversy. As the old saying goes, 'It was
ten miles into the woods and it's ten miles out.'

A democratic curriculum

The structures and processes discussed so far generally define
the quality of everyday life in schools. As part of the longstanding traditions and deep structures of the school, they also offer
powerful teachings about what and whom the school values.
For this reason, they constitute a kind of 'hidden' curriculum
by which people learn significant lessons about justice, power,
dignity, and self-worth. Democratizing these structures and
processes is a crucial aspect of the schools portrayed here, but
a more complete version also includes creative work towards
bringing democracy to the planned or overt curriculum.

Since democracy involves the informed consent of people, a
democratic curriculum emphasizes access to a wide range of
information and the right of those of varied opinion to have

their viewpoints heard. Educators in a democratic society have an obligation to help young people seek out a range of ideas and to voice their own. Unfortunately, many schools persistently shirk this obligation in several ways. First, they narrow the range of school-sponsored knowledge to what we might call 'official' or high-status knowledge that is produced or endorsed by the dominant culture (Apple 1993). Second, they silence the voices of those outside the dominant culture, particularly people of colour, women and, of course, the young. This observation can be substantiated with little more than a glance at textbooks, reading lists, and curriculum guides.

What is most disturbing is that all too many schools have taught this official, high-status knowledge as though it were 'truth' arisen from some immutable, infallible source. Those committed to a more participatory curriculum understand that knowledge is socially constructed, that it is produced and disseminated by people who have particular values, interests, and biases. This is simply a fact of life, since all of us are formed by our cultures, genders, geographies and so on. In a democratic curriculum, however, young people learn to be 'critical readers' of their society. When confronted with some knowledge or viewpoint, they are encouraged to ask questions like: Who said this? Why did they say it? Why should we believe this? and Who benefits if we believe this and act upon it?

To clarify this point, consider an example from a classroom observed by one of this book's editors. The teacher and students were engaged in a discussion of 'current events', using material from newspapers and focusing on 'natural disasters'. How we think about natural disasters and whose definition of what they are is crucial. For instance, we are now (unfortunately) quite used to seeing pictures of disasters in which thousands of people lose their lives to storms, drought, and so on. Like the children in that classroom, we are told to think of them as 'natural' disasters. But is this seemingly neutral way of understanding current events really neutral, or are particular values smuggled in or omitted in subtle ways?

Part of the discussion that went on in that classroom provides a powerful reminder of why such a question is important.

The students noted the massive mud slides that had recently occurred in South America; large numbers of people were killed or badly injured as torrential rains washed their houses down the mountainsides. Yet a closer examination reveals that little about this disaster was 'natural'. Every year in South America there are rains, and every year people die. This particular year, an entire side of the mountain gave way; the thousands of people living on it lost their lives. No one in the valleys – the safe and fertile land – died.

Poor families are forced to live on the dangerous hillsides because this is the only land left on which they can afford to eke out a meagre existence. People crowd onto the mountainsides because of poverty and historical land ownership patterns that are grossly unequal. Hence, the problem is not the yearly rain – a natural occurrence – but the unequal economic structures that allow a small minority of individuals to control the very lives of the majority of people in that region.

This altered and more complete understanding of the problem is rich in pedagogic and curricular possibilities. Helping students to understand the different ways this 'current event' could be interpreted, and the benefits to different groups of people each interpretation brings, could ultimately lead them to a richer and more ethically committed sensitivity to the societies around them (Apple 1990).

A mathematics class in an urban school provides another example of how questions are used in a democratic classroom. Students in this class were regularly given a word problem involving the cost of a monthly bus pass. They were asked to calculate whether it was cheaper to buy a monthly pass or to pay each time one went to and from work. In this particular instance, given the number of workdays that the problem writer specified, the correct answer was to pay each time. Yet built into this problem is a set of assumptions that have little bearing on the realities of these young people's lives or those of their parents.

The students knew this answer was simply wrong. After all, many of their parents worked two part-time jobs to support themselves and their families. These jobs were often at fast-food restaurants and were the only jobs available in that community after the factories had moved to take advantage of lower wages and tax breaks in other parts of the world. Thus, in the experience of these children, a person used the bus at least four times a day to get to and from work, work that was without benefits, was low paid and was often dead-end.

This curriculum was obviously more than a little biased and insensitive. But the teacher creatively used the bias, asking students to reflect on what was wrong with this example and to think about how mathematics helped them understand their own and their parents' daily lives. In essence, she asked them to answer a question similar to those we asked above: *From whose perspective are we seeing the world in this material?* (Ladson-Billings 1995). By weaving this question into the entire mathematics unit, she integrated mathematics into students' everyday lives, thus giving their work more of an impact than was ever possible in the supposedly neutral standard curriculum that was connected to the supposedly neutral standardized achievement tests that determined those young persons' futures.

At the very least, each of these examples points to the fact that someone's tradition, someone's construction of what is important to know and how it should be used, is always incorporated into our planned curriculum, often in hidden ways. As in the example of the mathematics class, however, a democratic curriculum seeks to move beyond the 'selective tradition' of knowledge and meanings endorsed by the dominant culture, towards a wider range of views and voices (Williams 1961; Apple 1990). In a democratic society, no one individual or interest group can claim sole ownership of possible knowledge and meaning. Likewise, a democratic curriculum includes not only what adults think is important, but also the questions and concerns that young people have about themselves and their world. A democratic curriculum invites young people to shed the passive role of knowledge consumers and assume the active role of 'meaning makers'. It recognizes that people acquire knowledge by both studying external sources and engaging in complex activities that require them to construct their own knowledge.

As we have previously seen, the democratic way of life engages the creative process of seeking ways to extend and expand the values of democracy. This process, however, is not simply a participatory conversation about just anything. Rather, it is directed towards intelligent and reflective consideration of problems, events, and issues that arise in the course of our collective lives. A democratic curriculum involves continuous opportunities to explore such issues, to imagine responses to problems, and to act upon those responses. For example, the curriculum includes learning experiences organized around problems and issues such as 'Conflict', 'The Future of Our Community', 'Justice', 'Environmental Politics' and so on.

Moreover, the disciplines of knowledge are not simply categories of 'high culture' for children to absorb and accumulate; they are sources of insight and information that might be brought to bear on problems of living, lenses through which to look at those issues that confront us (Beane 1993). It is this last point that we can use to understand, for example, how talk about curriculum integration needs to move beyond mere questions about how to connect present pieces of the curriculum to a larger conversation involving what those connections might be about. As Dewey (1938, p. 49) pointed out:

> What avail is it to win prescribed amounts of information about geography and history, to win ability to read and write, if in the process the individual loses his [sic] soul; loses his appreciation of things worthwhile, of the values to which these things are relative; if he loses desire to apply what he has learned and, above all, loses the ability to extract meaning from his future experiences as they occur.

Despite democratic claims about equal opportunity, many obstacles still block the path of non-privileged young people in our schools – for instance, the overuse of standardized tests. One of the historic problems of many progressive curriculum ideas (and one reason why they have often lacked support in non-privileged communities) is that they appear to de-emphasize the kind of official knowledge and skills that young people need to negotiate their way past the gatekeepers of socioeconomic access (Delpit 1986, 1988).

We previously noted that democratic schools are in part distinguished from other kinds of progressive schools in that they explicitly seek change in antidemocratic conditions in the school and society. Educators who work in democratic schools, however, are also acutely aware that such conditions, and the obstacles to larger access, must be reckoned with until they are changed. For this reason, a democratic curriculum seeks to help students become knowledgeable and skilled in many ways, including those required by the gatekeepers of socioeconomic access. In short, democratic educators live with the constant tension of seeking a more significant education for young people while still attending to the knowledge and skills expected by powerful educational forces whose interests are anything but democratic. Thus, we cannot ignore dominant knowledge. Having it does open some doors. But we must be careful in our interpretation here, because we do not want to endorse a continuation of the rigid 'drill and skill' programmes that so often constitute the school experiences of non-privileged children. These children, too, have a right to the best of our progressive ideas. Our task is to reconstruct dominant knowledge and employ it to help, not hinder, those who are least privileged in this society.

The matter of creating a democratic curriculum is almost certain to involve conflict and contention. Practically all that is included in this sketch comes up against much of the dominant and longstanding view of what the planned curriculum ought to be about. The possibility of hearing a wide range of views and voices is often seen as a threat to the dominant culture, especially since some of those voices offer interpretations of issues and events quite different from those traditionally taught in schools. Worse yet, encouraging young people to critically analyse issues and events raises the possibility that they might call dominant interpretations (and teachings) into question. The same is true for organizing the curriculum around major social problems and issues, but this arrangement also comes into conflict with the sterilized version of knowledge and skill that is part of the separate-subject, discipline-centred, 'high culture' approach to curriculum. Finally, the possibility that young people might contribute their own questions and concerns to the curriculum raises the threat of touching on issues that reveal the ethical and political contradictions that permeate our society and of detracting from the values this society says it upholds.

All of these sources of resistance have been encountered repeatedly by those committed to democratic schooling. The resistance is not always couched in clear and explicit terms, however. For example, there are those who say that young people should not take on social issues because they are not ready to understand the complexities involved or because they might become depressed. Such arguments, of course, entirely ignore the fact that the young are real people living out real lives in our society; many of them know all too well, from their own lived experiences, about the consequences of racism, poverty, gender bias, homelessness and so on. Obviously, then, those arguments simply seek to avoid the possibility that young people might come to see the political, ethical, and social contradictions that detract from their own dignity and seek to act against them.

It is important to note again that the concept of democratic schools is not intended only for the experiences of students. Adults, too, including professional educators, have a right to experience the democratic way of life in schools. We have already cited one example with regard to participation in determining policy and other decision making. But just as young people have a right to help create arrangements for their own education, so do teachers and other educators have a right to help create their own programmes for professional growth based upon their perceptions of problems and issues in their classrooms, schools and professional lives.

Furthermore, teachers have a right to have their voices heard in creating the curriculum, especially that intended for the particular young people they work with. Even the most casual of observers cannot help but notice that this right has been seriously eroded over the past several decades as curriculum decisions and even specific curriculum plans have been central-ized in state and district offices of education. The consequent 'de-skilling' of teachers, the redefinition of their work as the implementation of others' ideas and plans, is among the most obvious, and unbecoming, examples of how democracy has been dissolving in our schools (Apple 1986). Moreover, much of the talk about 'site-based management', while appearing to reverse such centralization, actually amounts to little more than localizing struggles over limited resources and accountability for policy and programme decisions made in distant places.

Finally, the matter of teachers' control of their own profes-sional work involves not just resources and curriculum man-dates, but instructional practices as well. Earlier we described how structural and curricular aspects of the school might be shaped by democratic values, though we also understand that they are also guided by research and other technical knowledge. In democratic schools, such knowledge does not come only from 'elite' sources located outside the school, such as aca-demic researchers. Of even more interest is the knowledge that teachers produce for their own use through action research and local dialogue. This does not mean other sources of profes-sional knowledge are invalid or useless; it simply means they are not the only sources of worthwhile ideas.

When we link the democratic right of teachers to exercise meaningful control over their own work with the obligation of teachers and other adults to extend the democratic way of life to young people, we see the real possibility that demo-cratic values might become a source of coherence for life in our schools. To turn the possibility into reality, however, we will again have to come up against some difficult questions. For instance, parents, the community, and the state certainly have a right to say what goals they want for education. But should they have the same say as professional educators in decisions about such matters as curriculum organization and resources? Does the heavy obligation to democracy that we have asked teachers to carry entitle them to certain professional autonomies beyond community control? What can the stories in this book tell us about such questions?

Building on a rich legacy

The picture we have sketched so far seems splendid in theory, but can it be fleshed out given present realities? It is true that the gap between democratic values and school practices is as wide now as it has ever been. But as the stories in this book reveal, the struggle to create democratic schools is alive in many places. The efforts described here are not anomalies of our own times; they are contemporary examples of a long line of work that has stretched over more than a century. As such, they offer a glimpse of the possibilities on the other side of the question that people today are still asking themselves: *How might schools both express and extend the meaning of democracy?*

We will read, for example, of serious efforts to connect the work of the school with the life of the community. Behind the projects described here lie movements that took place 50 and more years ago in places such as Baltimore (Maryland), Pulaski (Wisconsin) and Pasadena (California) – places where young people undertook projects to solve serious community problems (see, for example, Anderson and Young 1951). Like today's efforts, those earlier projects were not short-term activities, important as those might be, but sustained efforts to forge substantive links with communities.

We will also read of attempts to create space in the curriculum for the study of large-scale social problems. Here we can look back to some of the progressive schools involved in the famous Eight-Year Study of the 1930s (Aikin 1962) and to the many classroom stories that emerged from the 'core' movement in the 1940s and 1950s (see, for example, Faunce and Bossing 1951).[2]

We will look at cooperative learning, which was favoured in many of the earlier 'core' schools and in the child-centred programmes described by Rugg and Shumaker (1928) and the authors of *Life Skills in School and Society* (Rubin 1969). Our stories, like the earlier efforts, are concerned primarily with cooperative learning as a crucial aspect of the democratic way of life, not with the current popular focus of cooperative learning as a specific strategy for academic achievement.

In various ways, each story in this book emphasizes the involvement of young people in curriculum and other kinds of planning. The authors are following a long line of work describing such involvement not simply as a technique for reducing alienation and rebellion in classrooms but as part of a larger commitment to promoting individual and collective efficacy among young people (see, for example, Hopkins 1941; Giles, McCutchen and Zechiel 1942; Zapf 1959; Waskin and Parrish 1967).

These stories also speak of serious efforts to build on cultural diversity and to assuage the inequitable conditions surrounding cultural differences. In this regard, we should not forget that African Americans developed textbooks on their own history for segregated schools in the South during the 1930s and 1940s. So much of the work in this area stands on the shoulders of W.E.B. Du Bois, who relentlessly fought to elevate the status and expectations of education for blacks – for example, seeing in job-skill training programmes the obvious implications for differentiation of labour by race:

> The ideals of education, whether men are taught to teach or plow, to weave or to write, must not be allowed to sink into sordid utilitarianism. Education must keep broad ideals before it, and never forget that it is dealing with Souls and not with Dollars.

> (Du Bois 1902: 82)

We will hear the same theme resounding in the view of vocational education carried out at the Rindge School.

Nor are the authors here the first to recognize that creating democratic schools is a difficult endeavour when stronger currents outside the school seem to be flowing in the opposite direction. Rugg (1939) and others spoke to this issue in the midst of social efficiency movements during the industrial revolution. In addition, numerous authors of a considerable number of books and articles in the early 1950s – the notorious 'McCarthy era' in the United States of America – recounted chilling stories of ultraconservative attacks that resonate in our own times (see, for example, Cunningham 1952).

This brief historical sketch has focused mainly on the legacy of democratic education within schools. We would be remiss, however, if we failed to recognize that such work was (and still is) done in conjunction with efforts outside the schools themselves. For example, much of the impulse towards democratic schools rests on the prolific work of John Dewey, including not only that in education, such as his epic *Democracy and Education* (1916), but the vast array of essays and books on democracy in virtually all aspects of social affairs. A large debt is also owed to people like Elizabeth Harrison and Ella Flagg Young, who fought hard for the rights of children and teachers, and to others like George Counts and Harold Rugg, who advocated for a view of education as part of more widespread democratic social reconstruction.

Similarly, political activists in larger civil rights movements played no small part in democratizing various aspects of schooling. Were it not for their efforts, the schools might still be plagued by legally sanctioned racial segregation and exclusion of people with disabilities. As well, we cannot ignore the efforts of such groups as the American Library Association to protect young people from the restrictive limitations of censorship. While the courts are still confounded by the question of whether the school should be an arena for full democracy or a 'limited forum' for democratic rights, it is all too possible to imagine that the question itself might never have reached the courts were it not for the relentless appeals of democratic activists.

Clearly, then, the idea of extending and protecting democracy in schools is not simply a product of our own times. Both the general concept and the specific features we have sketched out have roots in efforts stretching back more than a century. The historian of democratic schools, however, always has to keep two things in mind. First, just as democracy has had multiple meanings in the larger society, so has its interpretation with regard to schools been somewhat ambiguous. Second, democracy is a dynamic concept that requires continuous examination in light of changing times. For these reasons, we are always at risk of being disappointed when one or another historical attempt at democratic schools did not push as far as we would wish or is revealed as a mix of success and contradiction. What is important is that we recognize moments of democratic impulse in the past as a legacy on which to build our own efforts.

Towards democratic schools

We have chosen to include in this book four examples of democracy brought to life in schools: Central Park East Secondary School in New York City, the Rindge School of Technical Arts in the Boston area, La Escuela Fratney in Milwaukee and a particular programme within Marquette Middle School (now called Georgia O'Keefe Middle School) in Madison, Wisconsin. Each represents the creative response of educators to the realities of poverty, injustice, and dislocation. All show the rich learning experiences that result from people's determination to make their classrooms centres of democratic practice and to create permeable boundaries between the school and the larger society.

Early on, we made a decision that these stories must be told in the words of the people involved. This is crucial. The feelings of frustration, and sometimes cynicism, that many educators and community members experience are often the result of not hearing each other's stories. Failure seems to make better headlines than hard-won, slow success. The stories presented here are not romantic. They are honest about the possibilities, and difficulties, we face as we move towards more democratic practices.

Let us remember who that 'we' is. Democratic schools need to be based on a broad definition of 'we', a commitment to building a community that is both of the school and of the society in which the school exists. Taken together, the stories told in this book say something quite important about the realities of democratic school reform. In each case, success required the conscious building of coalitions within the school and between the school and constituencies outside it. In none of the cases was the impetus generated from the 'top'. Instead, bottom-up movements – groups of teachers, the community, social activists, and so on – provided the driving force for change. Finally, none of the reforms was driven by a technical, achievement-at-all-costs vision, similar to the often largely rhetorical standards drives in all too many other countries. Instead, each was linked to a broadly defined set of values that was put into practice: enhancing participation at the grass roots and in the school, empowering individuals and groups who had heretofore been largely silenced, creating new ways of linking the real world and real social problems with the school so that the school is integrally connected to the experiences of people in their daily lives.

We shall be honest here. None of the examples included in this book is guaranteed to solve all the many problems schools confront. In fact, given the economic and social crises that continue to beset so many people in this society, schools and classrooms such as these have their work cut out for them, not only educationally but economically as well (see, for example, Kozol 1991). By attempting to create new, more democratic possibilities in our public schools, however, we can relearn what is possible. Make no mistake about it, the stakes are high, as James Mursell (1955, p. 3) pointed out 40 years ago:

> If the schools of a democratic society do not exist for and work for the support and extension of democracy, then they are either socially useless or socially dangerous. At the best they will educate people who will go their way and earn their living indifferent to the obligations of citizenship in particular and of the democratic way of life in general. . . . But quite likely they will educate people to be enemies of democracy – people who will fall prey to demagogues, and who back movements and rally round leaders hostile to the democratic way of life. Such schools are either futile or subversive. They have no legitimate reason for existence.

Notes

1 Rosa Parks was an African-American woman who was arrested in Montgomery, Alabama in 1955 for sitting in and refusing to leave the 'whites only' section on a municipal bus, as required by city segregation laws. This event triggered the Montgomery

bus boycott, a turning point in the Civil Rights movement in the United States and Rosa Parks became a national symbol of that struggle. One of the outcomes of that struggle was the establishment of Black History Month in schools, an annual event intended to foreground African-American life and achievements. Successful as that idea has proven to be, some critics have suggested that its widespread recognition as a single-month event has impeded efforts to more fully integrate African-American history and culture into the mainstream curriculum in US schools.

2 The Eight Year Study was a research project sponsored by the Progressive Education Association. The study explored how 30 high school faculties might organize the curriculum if they were freed from such constraints as college admission requirements. It examined how their graduates fared in college compared with graduates from traditional secondary schools. (All were guaranteed admission for the duration of the study.) In the end, graduates from those high schools that most dramatically broke with traditional curriculum arrangements fared better on almost every academic and affective measure used. Of note is the fact that those schools whose graduates fared best organized their programme around a 'core' curriculum based on a combination of adolescent needs and social issues similar to the 'integrated' curriculum used in some British schools. See, for example, Denis Gleeson and Geoff Whitty (1976) *Developments in Social Studies Teaching*. London: Open Books.

References

Aikin, Wilford (1962) *The Story of the Eight-Year Study*. New York: Harper and Brothers.

Anderson, Walter A. and Young, William E. (eds) (1951) *Action for Curriculum Improvement*. Washington, DC: ASCD.

Apple, Michael (1986) *Teachers and Texts: A Political Economy of Class and Gender Relations in Schools*. New York and London: Routledge and Kegan Paul.

Apple, Michael (1988) Redefining equality. *Teachers College Record*, 90: 167–84.

Apple, Michael (1990) *Ideology and Curriculum*, 2nd edn. New York: Routledge.

Apple, Michael (1993) *Official Knowledge: Democratic Education in a Conservative Age*. New York: Routledge.

Bastian, Ann, Fruchter, Norm, Gittell, Marilyn, Greer, Colin and Haskins, Kenneth (1986) *Choosing Equality: The Case for Democratic Schooling*. Philadelphia: Temple University Press.

Beane, James (1990) *Affect in the Curriculum*. New York: Teachers College Press.

Beane, James (1993) *A Middle School Curriculum: From Rhetoric to Reality*, 2nd edn. Columbus, OH: National Middle School Association.

Cunningham, Ruth (ed.) (1952) *Growing Up in an Anxious Age*. Washington, DC: ASCD.

Delfattore, Joan (1993) *Why Johnny Can't Read*. New Haven: Yale University Press.

Delpit, Lisa (1986) Skills and other dilemmas of a progressive black educator. *Harvard Educational Review*, 56: 379–85.

Delpit, Lisa (1988) The silenced dialogue: Power and pedagogy in educating other people's children. *Harvard Educational Review*, 58: 280–98.

Dewey, John (1916) *Democracy and Education*. New York: Macmillan.

Dewey, John (1938) *Experience and Education*. Bloomington, IN: Kappa Delta Pi.

Du Bois, W.E.B. (1902) *The Negro Artisan*. Atlanta: Atlanta University Press.

Faunce, Roland and Bossing, Nelson (1951) *Developing the Core Curriculum*. New York: Prentice-Hall.

Giles, H.H., McCutchen, S.F. and Zechiel, A.N. (1942) *Exploring the Curriculum*. New York and London: Harper and Brothers.

Graebner, William (1988) *The Engineering of Consent: Democracy as Social Authority in the Twentieth Century*. Madison: University of Wisconsin Press.

Greene, Maxine (1985) The role of education in democracy. *Educational Horizons*, 63 (special issue): 3–9.

Gutmann, Amy (1987) *Democratic Education*. Princeton, NJ: Princeton University Press.

Hopkins, L. Thomas (1941) *Interaction: The Democratic Process*. Boston: D.C. Heath.

Jensen, Carl and Project Censored (1994) *Censored: The News That Didn't Make the News – and Why*. New York: Four Walls Eight Windows.

Kozol, Jonathan (1991) *Savage Inequalities*. New York: Crown.

Ladson-Billings, Gloria (1995) Making math meaningful in cultural contexts, in Walter Secada, Elizabeth Fennema and Lisa Byrd-Adajian (eds) *New Directions in Equity for Mathematics Instruction*. New York: Cambridge University Press.

Mursell, James (1955) *Principles of Democratic Education*. New York: Norton.

Oakes, Jeannie (1985) *Keeping Track: How Schools Structure Inequality*. New Haven: Yale University Press.

Rubin, Louis J. (ed.) (1969) *Life Skills in School and Society*. Washington, DC: ASCD.

Rugg, Harold (ed.) (1939) *Democracy and the Curriculum. Third Yearbook of the John Dewey Society*. New York: D. Appleton-Century.

Rugg, Harold and Shumaker, Anne (1928) *The Child-Centered School*. New York: World Book.

Waskin, Yvonne and Parrish, Louise (1967) *Teacher-Pupil Planning for Better Classroom Learning*. New York: Pitman.

Williams, Raymond (1961) *The Long Revolution*. London: Chatto and Windus.

Wood, George (1988) Democracy and the curriculum, Landon Beyer and Michael Apple (eds) in *The Curriculum: Problems, Politics, and Possibilities*. Albany: State University of New York Press.

Wood, George (1992) *Schools That Work*. New York: Dutton.

Zapf, Rosalind (1959) *Democratic Practices in the Secondary School*. Englewood Cliffs, NJ: Prentice-Hall.

2

DEBORAH MEIER AND PAUL SCHWARZ

Central Park East Secondary School: The hard part is making it happen

Editors' introduction

Faced with the chilling effects of bureaucratic over-regulation, many secondary school educators have attempted to create space for more progressive, democratic, learner-centred schools. Still within the 'public' (that is, state supported) system, these have included both complete alternative schools and schools-within-schools that share resources with a comprehensive secondary school. In either case, these are almost always smaller than traditional schools and thus are better able to overcome the impersonal anonymity of large schools and construct more democratic communities of learning. In this chapter, Deborah Meier and Paul Schwarz describe perhaps the best known alternative secondary school in the United States of America, Central Park East Secondary School in New York City. In reading this chapter it is important to note that in addition to the 'habits of mind, work and heart' outlined here, Central Park East also prepares students at the school for a system of rigorous statewide examinations in various subjects.

Introduction

Central Park East Secondary School (CPESS), an alternative high school, expands on the successful learning environment created at the Central Park East Elementary Schools over the past 25 years. The secondary school is a cooperative project of Community School Board #4, the New York City Board of Education Alternative High School Division and the Coalition of Essential Schools, a national high school network.[1]

CPESS was started in the autumn of 1985 with 80 7th grade students. The school currently enrols 450 students in grades 7–12 and although CPESS will not grow larger, we have begun the creation of 11 new Coalition high schools in New York City. The students who attend CPESS are mostly neighbourhood (East Harlem) residents. Eighty-five per cent of the students are African American or Latino, and more than 20 per cent are eligible for service provided by special education. From careful tracking of our students, even when they move and attend other schools, we know that 97.3 per cent of the students who have attended CPESS graduate from high school and 90 per cent of those graduates attend college.

The fundamental aim of CPESS is to teach students to use their minds well, to prepare them for a well-lived life that is productive, socially useful, and personally satisfying. The school's academic programme stresses intellectual achievement and emphasizes the mastery of a limited number of centrally important subjects. This programme goes hand-in-hand with an approach that emphasizes learning how to learn, how to reason and how to investigate complex issues that require collaboration and personal responsibility.

The final high school diploma is not based on time spent in class or Carnegie units, but on each student's clear demonstration of achievement through the presentation of 14 portfolios to a graduation committee.[2] The school's values include high expectations, trust, a sense of personal decency, and respect for diversity. The school is open to all students and expects a great deal from each student.

The school is guided by the principles of the Coalition of Essential Schools, a national organization of high schools directed by Ted Sizer. The Coalition's principles include:

1 *Less is more.* It is more important to know some things well than to know many things superficially.
2 *Personalization.* Although the course of study is unified and universal, teaching and learning are personalized. No teacher is responsible for teaching more than 80 students (40 at CPESS) or advising more than 15.
3 *Goal setting.* High standards are set for all students. Students must clearly exhibit mastery of their school work.
4 *Student as worker.* CPESS teachers 'coach' students, encouraging them to find answers and, in effect, to teach themselves. Thus, students discover answers and solutions and learn by doing rather than by simply repeating what textbooks (or teachers) say.

Habits of mind, work and heart

It was Friday, May 2, 1992. Our students had spent the week talking, organizing and dealing with powerful feelings in the wake of the Rodney King verdict and the riots in Los Angeles. As luck would have it, an all-white choir from a small Michigan town was scheduled to sing for us that day. While LA was burning, and probably scared to death, the choir faced an audience of mostly African-American and Latino teenagers, many still brimming with eagerness to protest. There was tension in the air as one of our seniors stepped up to ask if he could say a few words that he thought might help.

'I took it on myself to come up here and talk to all you students about what we've been going through. I know from the Senior Institute that a lot of students have been talking about what's been going on in LA, and it bothers them a lot.

'I just wanted to tell you that no one here is our enemy . . . and that we have to stick together.

'. . . and that there's lots of people from . . . Michigan, right?' The students laugh. 'Michigan, not California, right?' There is more laughter from students.

'What they are doing here, they are doing for us. They are not here to make us feel better. They are here because they like to sing, and they're here to show us what they've got.

'They are not our enemies either. There is no one in this room that is our enemy. If we can stick together and stay with each other, we can show these people that we are not falling apart like some other people are.' Cheers and whoops fill the room.

'You got to do what you got to do, but showing your anger at these people here isn't going to do anything for any of us.'

If the primary public responsibility and justification for tax-supported schooling is raising a generation of fellow citizens, then the school – of necessity – must be a place where students learn the habits of mind, work and heart that lie at the core of such a democracy.

Since you cannot learn to be good at something you have never experienced – even vicariously – then it stands to reason that schools are a good place to experience what such democratic habits might be. It is as simple as that, and as complex. You cannot learn to play a game you have never seen played. No one would think of raising up musicians without being sure to place them in the company of musicians, including some at the top of their art.

Our task at CPESS was to take this idea seriously once again, and return the business of rearing our young to such basic principles. Instead of placing students in cohorts of equal ignorance and creating settings in which no expert ever performed his or her craft in the presence of novices and in which no one, novice or expert, ever showed what they could do, but only talked about it, we tried to turn the tables on it all.

We would keep the idea of kindergarten, where we both began our careers, going all the way through high school – and long after, we hoped. We wanted a schoolhouse that was naturally organized to be interesting, just like a good kindergarten room. We wanted a place where young people and their teachers could work in shared ways around topics and materials they were inclined to enjoy, for long stretches of time, and without too many preconceived strictures. We wanted opportunities for the least expert to watch and observe the more expert, and then to practise at their own pace. We wanted settings in which people knew each other through each other's works, through the close observation of actual practice – by our teacher colleagues and our student colleagues. A truly collegial setting.

So, we knew we had to be small, multi-aged, intimate and interesting. Family and school would need to be allies, as the two institutions responsible for shared child-rearing tasks. Between us, we had to find ways to make the idea of growing up seem wonderful and enticing, and noticeably varied enough to include everyone. We had to make the idea of being a powerful citizen on an ever broadening platform, with the capacity to play effective roles both in public and private, seem feasible and imaginable and appealing.

That is what good schooling could do. But it meant taking apart all this large and wordy rhetoric and finding the details that counted, just as we had both done when daily we set about putting together our kindergarten classrooms, from the block corner to the sand table, the selection of particular books, the organizing of pencils and paints, the placement of works of art, always with particular children in mind, always with particular purposes in mind.

So we put together CPESS, over time, collectively, modifying as we went, mindful of all the details of a place filled with many stories as well as common purposes. We created a structure in which people – students and students, students and teachers, and teachers and teachers, and their families – could think aloud together and jointly make decisions. We had to define what 'using your mind well', the Coalition of Essential School's overarching mission, meant. What were the habits of mind that defined a democratic citizen? We thought of friends who were 'good citizens' and tried to imagine what it was that they had in common. Surely it was not the ability to recall some body of facts or information, although they were curious about such mundane details. The two qualities that seemed to define our ideal citizen were *empathy* and *scepticism*: the ability to see a situation from the eyes of another and the tendency to wonder about the validity of what we encountered.

Our operational definition of a thoughtful person, a person whom we would be proud to claim as a graduate of our school, was one who could demonstrate to us, in a variety of ways and in numerous disciplines, that he or she was in the habit of tackling the following five questions:

1 How do you know what you know? (Evidence)
2 From whose viewpoint is this being presented? (Perspective)
3 How is this event or work connected to others? (Connections)
4 What if things were different? (Supposition)
5 Why is this important? (Relevance)

We have organized our curriculum and our assessment around the idea that a person in the habit of looking for answers to these five questions when presented with a novel situation is using his or her mind well. The nuances, the vocabulary, the tools change from physics to literature to geometry and so on. If these questions are the right ones, however, they ought also to apply to the playground and the workplace. Of course, such habits are neither learned nor used in a vacuum. They are embedded in appropriate subject matter; they depend on the ability of the learner to use skills of reading, writing, logic, computation, research and scientific inquiry to give them substance. But we hold to the concept of their universality across subject matter and age. A person in the habit of asking these five questions is a thoughtful person.

In fact, the biggest step we took was deciding that a student would graduate CPESS almost entirely on the basis of evidence of such thoughtfulness, over and over again in 14 designated fields of work. We called this Graduation by Portfolio, although our portfolios are compilations not merely of written work, but of everything and anything students believe speaks to their meeting the graduation standards we have spelled out.

The 14 portfolio areas: An overview for students and parents

The primary responsibility of the Senior Institute student is to complete the 14 portfolio requirements listed below.

These portfolios reflect cumulative knowledge and skill in each area as well as the specific CPESS habits of mind and work. Students will present the work in all 14 portfolio areas to their Graduation Committee for review and acceptance. They will meet for a full review of their seven chosen 'majors' to present, discuss and defend their work. There are, therefore, two stages to keep in mind: (1) preparation of the portfolio materials in collaboration with the adviser and others, and (2) presentation and defence of the materials. In some cases, portfolio work will need to be expanded, modified and represented for final approval. Students may also choose to present work a second time to earn a higher assessment.

It is important to remember that a majority of the work done in connection with a portfolio can and should be the outcome of the courses, seminars, internships and independent study that a student has engaged in during the normal course of his or her Senior Institute years. In addition, some of the material may be an outgrowth of work initiated in Divisions I or II or, where appropriate (for example, the Language Other Than English portfolio), work completed prior to entering the Senior Institute.

Portfolios include work in 14 areas: seven 'majors' and seven 'minors'. There is no one way to complete these requirements, nor one way to present them. People are different, and the individual portfolio will reflect these differences. The term 'portfolio' covers all the ways in which a student exhibits his or her knowledge, understanding, and skill. CPESS recommends interdisciplinary studies wherever possible, so work completed to meet one requirement may be used to fulfill other requirements as well.

While the final review is based on individual accomplishment, almost all portfolio requirements can be based on work done in collaboration with others, including group presentations. Such collaborative work is encouraged, since it often enables a student to engage in a much more complex and interesting project.

Quality and depth of understanding, good use of CPESS's five habits of mind and the capacity to present competent and convincing evidence of mastery as relevant to each particular field are the major criteria used by the Graduation Committee; however, portfolio work must reflect a concern for both substance and style. For example, written work must be submitted in clear, grammatical English that reflects the expected proficiency level of a high-school graduate in spelling, grammar and legibility. Errors should be eliminated before the portfolio is presented to the committee. Written work must generally be submitted in typewritten form. The same care in preparation and presentation applies to all other forms of work. Portfolio work should represent a student's best effort. The same holds true for the manner of presentation.

Different characteristics are more or less relevant to each portfolio area. Each academic discipline, for example, has developed its own 'scoring grid' to help students and Graduation Committee members focus objectively on the appropriate criteria. Over time, the criteria for acceptable performance will be more fully developed through both the creation of new scoring grids and the compilation of past student work that demonstrates accepted levels of skill. Students are expected to become familiar with the criteria by which they are measured (both the scoring grids and former student work).

At Graduation Committee meetings, students should be prepared to discuss not only the content of the portfolio, but their computer knowledge and growth in particular fields of work.

The following are the 14 Portfolio areas:

1 Postgraduate Plan
2 Science/Technology*
3 Mathematics*
4 History and Social Studies*
5 Literature*
6 Autobiography
7 School and Community
   Service and Internship
8 Ethics and Social Issues
9 Fine Arts/Aesthetics
10 Practical Skills
11 Media
12 Geography
13 Language Other Than English/
   Dual Language Proficiency
14 Physical Challenge

Senior project

One of the above portfolio topics or items will be separately assessed as a final Senior project. Each student is required to make a major presentation in 7 of the 14 areas described above. These include the four asterisked portfolios, and at least three others chosen in cooperation with the adviser. Grades of Distinguished, SatPlus, Sat, or MinSat will be used to grade work as a whole. In the seven 'minor' portfolios, a student will be graded pass/fail. Passing will be upon recommendation of the adviser and approval of the full Graduation Committee.

The student may, however, request a grade from the adviser (Distinguished, SatPlus, etc.). In this case, the student must provide the committee with sufficient time to review all relevant materials and to discuss the recommended grade at a meeting of the committee. Such a grade would be subject to approval by the entire committee.

We invented graduation committees, which are a little like doctoral committees. Each committee includes at least two faculty members, an adult of the student's choice, and another student member. Their job is to read, review, observe, listen to the evidence and make appropriate recommendations for revision or approval. When we started, it was hard for us to imagine such a process, but today stories like the one below reinforce our commitment to this time-consuming process.

A meeting of the graduation committee

It is a warm Friday afternoon in September and Monique's graduation committee has convened for the first time. As we wait for Monique's mother to arrive (each student is allowed to choose one adult, and Monique has chosen her mother – according to local wisdom, always a risky choice). Monique is so nervous she cannot sit still. 'I've got to go to the bathroom', she says, and makes her third trip in the last 15 minutes.

Finally, we all settle in around a table in my office and Monique begins her presentation. She has chosen to present a paper on AIDS discrimination in health care. She refers to her paper, but only occasionally. At the start, she is somewhat ashen-faced. She sits bolt upright, as opposed to her usual adolescent slump, and begins nearly every sentence with 'I put . . .' – as in 'I put in an interview with a nurse who works in the emergency room to describe the feelings of a professional whose primary responsibility is not AIDS-related.'

Monique finishes her presentation and asks if there are any questions. She knows there will be. This is the part of the meeting where committee members probe to see if she has acquired our five habits of mind, the hallmark of a CPESS graduate. We begin gently asking her for the source of some of her information. She handles these questions easily. Students always discuss committee experiences with their friends and Monique expected questions about sources.

However, the questions quickly become less predictable. 'Monique', I ask, 'you spoke of doctors who screened patients

for the HIV virus without their knowledge or permission. You
see this as a bad thing, an invasion of their privacy. Just last
Sunday I saw a TV program about Cuba and their response to
the AIDS epidemic. In Cuba they test everyone. They don't ask
permission. When they find an HIV-positive person, they quar-
antine them. They are put in a comfortable place with good
food and excellent health care, but they must stay there. Period. One result is that they have greatly lessened the spread of
the disease. What if they were to do that here?'

Monique is on her own here. She certainly did not anticipate this question, and she cannot begin her answer with 'I put'.
But something happens to her at that moment; a physical
change takes place, one that I have often seen at a graduation
committee meeting. Monique does not hesitate. She straightens
up, leans forward, looks me right in the eye, and says, 'My father
died of AIDS and that's why I decided to present this portfolio
first. It is real important to me.'

She continues, 'I would be in favor of anything that pre-
vents AIDS or even slows it down a little bit, but I don't know
about not telling people that you are testing them. I can see
both sides of the question and I don't want to decide. I think
we should take a vote.'

'Who should vote?' I ask.

'Everyone', she answers immediately. 'Even little kids. This
is so important that everyone should be able to vote.'

The committee meeting ends after an hour of presentation
and questions. Committee members fill out grids that we have
created here at CPESS: one to assess the major project in the
portfolio (our portfolios are compilations of work) and a tabulation form that gives a grade for this portfolio, her first of seven
major portfolios.

As I announce the grade to Monique – a better than satisfact-
ory grade – and give her our feedback on what we thought was
strong in her work and what we thought might have improved
the portfolio, she grins from ear to ear. She is back to her
younger self. She can hardly listen to us and immediately
excuses herself to go and talk to Yuiza and Frances, her best
friends, who are waiting in the lobby for her.

I put papers and forms and tabulation sheets away and prepare for my next graduation committee. Carlos is presenting his literature portfolio – or rather, he is presenting himself as a person in the habit of using his mind well, of using our habits of mind, and he is going to demonstrate these qualities through his work in the field of literature.

After school, I meet some school friends and they ask me why I am so 'high'. It is because occasionally, during committee meetings like Monique's, I witness the fruits of our work together. I see the hidden hours of struggle that so many teachers and parents and students have invested in learning. The committee meetings are not only our final assessment, they are often 'payoff time', a concrete reward for having studied and read and written and argued and thought so long and so hard.

Once in a while I see magic. Not sleight-of-hand magic, but the magic of a child's first step or her first word. Magic that has been earned. The magic of students growing up as thinkers, gaining confidence, showing off their minds – of a young person changing, in front of my eyes, into a woman who is confident, thoughtful and competent.

The choices we have made

How did we create graduation committees as rigorous and as personal as the one described above? How did we create a school organization that allows teachers to attend to details, the way early childhood teachers do? The changes we have made are not simple. They have forced us to make weighty choices and there have been sacrifices involved in each of them.

Half-day, theme-centred classes

First, we shall discuss teacher : student ratios. CPESS offers a common core curriculum for all students in grades 7–10, organized around two major fields: maths/science for half the school day and humanities (art, history, social studies, and literature) for the other half.

Each class is centred around a theme. Here, for example, are two themes of study, one in humanities and one in maths/ science, both taken from the curriculum of our Division II, 9th and 10th grades:

The first is *Justice: Systems of Laws and Government*. At least two very different concepts of justice are explored in this year-long theme: one consensual and the other adversarial. Ideas of fairness, conflict resolution and equity are examined in these two societies. The American justice system and critical legal landmarks are examined in detail. Students develop first-hand experience with the preparation and defence of a legal brief. They explore the jury system and the nature of evidence. The essential questions in the study are: How is authority justified? How are conflicts resolved? Are justice, morality and fairness synonymous?

The second, *Motion and Forces of Energy*, is a two-year theme driven by the following essential questions: How do things move? How does energy behave in its different forms? Is energy ever made or lost? In the investigation of these questions, students work on projects such as designing and analysing an original amusement park ride or doing a scientific analysis of a projectile (for example, a basketball or a javelin in flight). They used a variety of commercially produced computer software to model and analyse projectile motion and collisions of two or more bodies. The theme includes an emphasis on the scientific method and the techniques of statistics and probability. Students also investigate the mathematical themes of counting, measuring, locating and describing, which lead them to a more intense study of algebra, geometry, trigonometry, mathematical transformations, vectors, and matrices.

In grades 7–10, each class period is two hours long, and each teacher teaches two classes a day rather than the five classes that are common in many other schools. This change has meant a reconceptualization of instructional practice. Two-hour classes push teachers to use a variety of strategies, such as whole-group instruction, small-group collaborative work, library research and hands-on problem solving. The teacher cannot bore children by lecturing them for two hours at a time.

Instruction in the Senior Institute – our name for grades 11 and 12 – works a little differently. Students in this transitional stage spend more time taking courses out of our building: at colleges and museums, at internships and in independent study. A substantial portion of their day is also spent with their advisers, preparing for graduation and the steps beyond.

Small classes

A second priority is to reduce not only the number of classes taught, but also class size. To accomplish this goal, we have chosen to concentrate the great bulk of the resources allotted to us in core classroom instruction. As we have grown from a single 7th grade class in 1985 to our full complement in 1995, we have made the ratio of students to teachers our priority. We have no guidance counsellors, no gym teacher (although we do have an extensive intramural programme and a substantial after-school athletics programme), no music teacher and a single art teacher for the whole school. We have no department chairs, no deans and one social worker; in return for class sizes of under 20, other teachers have assumed many of the functions traditionally carried out by these personnel. All professional staff are advisers to a group of under 15 students for two years. This group meets for several hours each week and it is the adviser who has long-range, in-depth relationships with each student's family.

Critical friends

Powerful as this educational process is, it puts us at odds with ideas of curriculum and assessment that stress memorization and coverage. This kind of learning is personal; it requires internalizing, not just saying, difficult ideas. It assumes an active role by the learner and, like other creative acts, it is unpredictable and full of surprises. No textbooks or standardized tests exist for teaching this way. Adults must work together to constantly re-create curriculum, invent new forms for exhibiting knowledge and decide when the school is ready to say, 'She's done it. It's time to hand her a diploma.' Such chutzpah requires that standards be constantly discussed and agreed on.

External colleagues, what we call 'critical friends', are essential to help us look critically at the school's work. 'Autonomy' cannot be synonymous with privacy. Quite the opposite. CPESS, and its work, are always public. We bring in experts of various sorts several times a year to help us set standards and examine our curriculum. For instance, professors from local colleges and universities have come to our school and reviewed the writing quality of portfolio items, in almost all cases confirming our staff's own evaluations of the items. We have even had critical friends join us for a full day of graduation portfolio review. These teachers from traditional public schools in New York City, state education department employees, principals of comprehensive high schools, principals and teachers from our sister schools, foundation representatives and outside experts looked at portfolios of differing quality, talked to students about their studies and watched videotapes of student presentations. They also met with us and with teachers, offering thought-provoking comments, criticisms and advice on a range of topics, from the structure of our school to academic requirements. By opening our programme to this kind of outside scrutiny, we hold ourselves accountable to the public while also providing rich collaborative experiences for the staff.

Time for planning, collaboration and assessment

To make such collaboration possible we had to address another priority: teacher time. We had to build into the professional life of teachers time for adults to do this new kind of planning, collaboration and assessment. Every Monday, staff meet from 3.00 pm to 4.30 pm. On Friday, we have classes from 8.00 am to 1.00 pm, and the staff meet again from 1.30 pm until 3.00 pm. This is three hours a week that staff work together on whole-school issues. Some of that time is used by vertical teams (all the humanities teachers and all the maths/science teachers) to meet and discuss scope and sequence and standards of work from 7th grade through to graduation. At least once a month, our whole staff gather to discuss issues of race, class and gender. Also once a month, we gather to consider school matters such as family conferences, report writing or reports and recommendations from various working subgroups. Several times a year, we meet over weekends for public review of students' work and developing curriculum. We have even raised some funds to pay teachers a stipend for working during July on collaborative projects.

In addition, each week we have carved out a three-hour block of time for teams of teachers who work with the same students to meet. We have done this by requiring that each student in grades 7–10 have a community service placement. We have one teacher who is responsible for these placements. We organize the placements so that students who go into the community to work do so in constellations of 80 students per day. This arrangement frees teams of teachers to work together for that half day. The students check in with their adviser at 9.00 am and then go to their placement. They return at noon and go to lunch and midday options (gym, library, etc). Their teachers have until 1.00 pm to plan collaboratively and the students have rich opportunities for using their minds in a wide variety of institutions, from day-care classrooms to museums, hospitals and homes for the aged.

These formal and informal gatherings that take place all day long are where 'staff development' occurs. They are where the newest teacher learns his or her trade, and senior staff re-examine and revisit old issues. While everyone complains occasionally of being exhausted – and so we skip a meeting here and there – we do not complain of burnout. We are never treated like appliances, but are in control of our own profession.

Through these varied forms of face-to-face meetings, the governance of the school is enacted. Decisions are made, wherever possible, by those who must implement them. But decisions also belong to the wider community of staff, parents and students, and they have always the right to ask that a decision be reconsidered, defended and explained. In these open and accessible ways, staff and students learn about the complexities of democracy. They learn of its limitations and of the realities of institutional trade-offs, and they imagine how they might even do it better. We ourselves are forever tinkering with ways to govern better (and less), using the same habits of mind we ask of our students.

Altered perceptions

We come back to the personal (as former kindergarten teachers, we could not do otherwise), which includes looking at children as members of their family and reflecting on how schooling has altered both children's and family's perceptions of themselves. One mother described to an audience of teachers how this kind of schooling has changed her family; her words convey what it is we hope for from our schooling:

> As we (our family) became familiar with the process of presenting work for criticism to a supportive group of peers, we all became involved with it.
>
> I remember when Zawadi (my middle daughter) was doing a portfolio item on Philip Parnell, a case of a teenager who was shot down and killed by a police officer in New Jersey. I went to the library with her and we did extensive research. She told me what to look for.
>
> She interviewed my brother, who is a NYC police officer, so she could get a feeling for what a police officer feels like when something like that happens. She didn't want her exhibition to be biased . . .
>
> I watched her formulate her questions. I watched her interview people. I watched her over a period of several years pull all that information into a play that she decided to use as a vehicle for her presentation.
>
> And then I watched her have her friends from school come to my living room. I watched her become the director. And I watched her listen to them – to take into account how they felt – how they would have responded in that case.

My son chose to focus on his experience as a child living in three different states and how they impacted on who he has become.

This having to define himself was insightful to us all. His accounts of specific instances of racism were validated by his sisters and led to family discussions about those instances and how they could be empowering if you change the anger to strength.

My youngest daughter has taken to documenting the family history, which has brought into the picture the total United States history and the history of the Caribbean. She has had to do extensive research around those oral histories, which are important to me because I grew up with them but never thought to document them. This process allowed her to do that and to give her the time so that she wasn't doing the rote kind of work our children used to do, but she was placing her time in something that was meaningful and important to her and she was excited about that.

The history of progressive education has largely been written in schools for young children – in kindergartens and early childhood centres and Head Start centres. Its spokespeople have been professionals who have studied and practised their craft with the young: Maria Montessori, Jean Piaget, John Dewey, Lillian Weber and Barbara Biber, and so many other teachers who have gone before. They created schools where what students studied was intimately connected to their lives and where people had a chance to work and learn side by side. Our success at CPESS is to re-create those structures and to implement goals in settings where older students learn. It is also our challenge.

We have created a structure where it is possible to learn to know students well so they can learn to use their minds well; we have created a structure where teachers can be in responsible control of their professional lives and where there is a strong professional community supporting them; we have created an assessment system that can hold students to high standards without standardization; we have created a curriculum structure based on habits of mind that focus on tools for thinking, not just bits and pieces of information. That is the easy part; the hard part is making it happen.

Notes

1 The Coalition of Essential Schools is a national network of schools attempting to implement progressive pedagogical ideas. School participation is voluntary and control of the schools remains with each local school community. This should *not* be confused with networks of for-profit schools run by private companies such as The Edison Project or Educational Alternatives Incorporated. The latter, EAI, is similar to the idea of 'education action zones' now being instituted in the UK. These ideas have been widely criticized in the USA and have been less than successful. For a critique of these kinds of programmes as they have emerged in the United States, see Alex Molnar (1996) *Giving Kids the Business: The Commercialization of America's Schools*. Oxford: Westview.
2 Carnegie Units are nationally standardized amounts of 'credits' collected by secondary school students based on the amount of time spent in particular subject courses. For example, a student successfully completing a one semester/term course in History would receive one-half Carnegie Unit, while a full-year course would involve a full unit. Various states and communities require that a certain number of Carnegie Units be accrued by students in order to receive a high-school diploma. Critics of the system point out that such credits are based solely on 'seat-time' and inhibit flexibility in the curriculum schedule.

3

LARRY ROSENSTOCK AND ADRIA STEINBERG

Beyond the shop: Reinventing vocational education

Editors' introduction

The separation of academic and vocational studies has served a variety of anti-democratic purposes such as maintaining the status of 'high culture' over that of everyday life and segregating mostly non-privileged youth deemed to be destined for the trades from those youth – mostly from privileged backgrounds – who are deemed to be destined for university and the professions. In this chapter, Larry Rosenstock and Adria Steinberg, respectively Director and Academic Coordinator of the Rindge School of Technical Arts in Cambridge, Massachusetts, describe how one school has moved beyond the traditional dualism of academic and vocational studies and its effects. Rejecting the simplistic definition of democracy as consumer choice, the faculty at Rindge has constructed a programme that involves students in projects, which address community needs, empowers faculty to make important curriculum decisions and integrates academic and vocational knowledge through community-centred projects. Successful as the programme has been, it has also been subjected to criticisms from those who have historically benefited from the class privileges accruing in traditional school arrangements.

Vocational education straddles a fundamental contradiction. On the one hand it has long been, and still is, a means of providing an education to students who would not otherwise attend school. On the other hand, it has created a dual system in which lower income students are tracked into vocational classes and away from the academic courses that prepare other students for further education and higher income, white-collar jobs.

The Rindge School of Technical Arts opened in 1888 as the first public vocational high school in Massachusetts, and the second in the United States. Built with funds provided by a local industrialist named Frederick Rindge, the school still displays his sentiments, carved in granite over the front door: 'Work is one of our greatest blessings. Everyone should have an honest occupation.' Frederick Rindge acted out of a democratic impulse, yet helped create a mechanism for the 'sorting of students by their evident and probable destinies' (Carnoy and Levin 1985, p. 94).

The groundwork for Rindge's generous bequest had been laid 50 years earlier in Massachusetts, when the State Board of Education, led by Horace Mann, argued that the Common School system should be expanded to bring together in the schools children from all backgrounds. Concerned that many rural and working-class families still did not send their children to school, local boards sought to differentiate the types of schools available. The introduction of vocational schools with agricultural and mechanical programmes was described as providing a practical reason for Irish immigrant and rural students to attend.

By the 1880s and 1890s, secondary schools were increasingly viewed as avenues to middle management jobs in the new industrial firms. Aware of the increasing strength of organized labour, the business sector sought to create programmes that would train students in the new technical skills needed by industry, instil in them attitudes of loyalty to their employers and socialize them for an industrial economy. Thus emerged

in Massachusetts the first dual system: one to educate middle-
and upper-level managers, the other to train labourers and
clerical workers.

Despite criticism of the narrow, utilitarian nature of vocational education, it continued to spread, advocated by the newly
formed National Association of Manufacturers and opposed
initially by organized labour. A 1906 report by the Massachusetts Commission on Industrial and Technical Education triggered a debate between John Dewey and David Snedden, the
Commissioner of Education in Massachusetts. While Snedden
defended the efficiency of the dual system, Dewey saw the
segregated vocational education favoured by business as a 'form
of class education which would make the schools a more effi-
·cient agency for the reproduction of an undemocratic society'
(Westbrook 1991, p. 175). Dewey viewed the issue of vocational
education as central to the future of democracy; his framing of
the issue still resonates strongly today:

> Its [vocational education's] right development will do more
> to make public education truly democratic than any other
> agency now under consideration. Its wrong treatment will
> as surely accentuate all undemocratic tendencies in our
> present situation, by fostering and strengthening class divi-
> sions in school and out. . . . Those who believe in the con-
> tinued existence of what they are pleased to call the 'lower
> classes' or the 'laboring classes' would naturally rejoice to
> have schools in which these 'classes' would be segregated.
> And some employers of labor would doubtless rejoice
> to have schools, supported by public taxation, supply
> them with additional food for their mills. . . . [Everyone
> else] should be united against every proposition, in what-
> ever form advanced, to separate training of employees from
> training for citizenship, training of intelligence and char-
> acter from training for narrow, industrial efficiency.
>
> (Dewey 1993)

Although there was deep disagreement about the direction
of vocational education, it nevertheless had wide support. A

powerful lobbying organization, the National Society for the Promotion of Industrial Education, was supported by a broad range of groups, including educators, the Chamber of Commerce, the National Association of Manufacturers, the American Federation of Labor (sensing the inevitability of vocational education, labour wanted a voice in redirecting its anti-union bias), major farm organizations and settlement workers.

The campaign culminated in the passage of the Smith-Hughes Act in 1917, which began the federal support for vocational education that has continued until the present. The fundamental contradiction of vocational education was set: while it profoundly transformed the rate of Massachusetts high school enrolment from a mere 6.7 per cent of 14–17-year-olds in 1888 to 32.3 per cent of that population by 1906 (Krug 1969, p. 220, quoting the 1906 Report of the Massachusetts Commission on Industrial and Technical Education), it became a separate, second-class system under separate control. (Dewey's advocacy of a single system won a Pyrrhic victory: vocational education was incorporated into the public school system, but as a distinct track within that system.)

The segregation of vocational education was further reinforced by two other concomitant factors. The first, the compulsory education laws of 1923, captured many students into vocational programmes who were now required to go to school. At the same time, 'intelligence tests' such as the intelligence quotient (IQ) and Binet were developed and used to channel students towards either vocational or academic concentrations.

By the time of the authorization of the Carl D. Perkins Vocational Education and Applied Technology Act of 1990, Congress was receptive to the idea of substantially reshaping vocational education. Widespread dissatisfaction with the job entrance rates and wage rates of vocational school graduates, combined with strong pressure from a coalition of national advocacy groups led by the Center for Law and Education, galvanized support for change.[1] With only 27 per cent of all vocational school graduates working for even a single day in a job related to their vocational training (*National Assessment of Vocational Education* 1987), the time had come to move away from narrow skills training for specific occupations to broad instruction in 'all aspects of the industry'.[2]

Just over a century after its founding, Rindge was poised, once again, to play a leading role in defining vocational education. We had a veteran faculty, a new executive director (Larry Rosenstock, a former carpentry teacher at Rindge, returning after two years as a staff attorney for the Center for Law and Education), a new academic co-ordinator (Adria Steinberg) and the full support of Mary Lou McGrath, the superintendent of the Cambridge Public Schools, who instructed us to comply with the Perkins Act and to 'turn the program upside down and inside out' in order to do so. It was our task to help the faculty put the rhetoric of Perkins and the progressivism of Dewey into daily practice at Rindge.

CityWorks

Some people seem to have a problem with the Rindge School of Technical Arts. They are always putting RSTA down and stereotyping us: . . . the students in RSTA are dumb; they will not go to college; they are going to drop out. Well, I will not take this anymore! . . . Being a freshman in RSTA, I am positive that I will go to college, and a lot of my confidence has come from my teachers. RSTA students have worked hard, demonstrated enthusiasm, and displayed some great exhibits. We are smart, not only in mind, but also with our hands. We have, or will have shortly, an advanced technological mind as well as an academic mind. . . . We give respect, so we expect respect. Success demands it!

In March 1993, Paulina Mauras published this statement in our high school newspaper. Her anger is not surprising. As a 9th grade student in the vocational wing of Cambridge's comprehensive high school, Paulina suffers from the low status accorded to vocational education and all who enter it.

What is worth noting is that this 14-year-old is ready to do something about it. She is acting the way one would hope all members of a participatory democracy could act: speaking out publicly in protest of something she sees as unfair, challenging class stereotypes, showing confidence in herself and her working-class peers and seeing herself as a member of a community.

Paulina's notion of combining hands and mind, and the development of her skills in doing so, come directly from her experiences in CityWorks, the centrepiece of the 9th grade programme at Rindge. Cambridge is the 'text' as students investigate the neighbourhoods, the systems, the people and the needs that compose an urban community. Students work on individual and group projects, bringing aspects of their community into the classroom by creating numerous 'artefacts' of Cambridge: maps, photographs, tapes, oral histories and three-dimensional models.

Several features make this programme unusual. First, CityWorks combines key characteristics of vocational programmes – a project approach, apprentice–master relationships, and real clients – with the broader content and essential skills of academic education. Projects involve hands-on work, like making a wall-size map of the city and wiring it to light up selected landmarks. At the same time, students engage in problem solving, like deciding where on the map to locate a new centre for teenagers that would attract youth from all ethnic and racial communities of the city.

Second, CityWorks is taught in a space designed for collaborative project work. Looking for an alternative to both shops and classrooms, we borrowed the notion of 'studios' from design schools. There is an open area at one end of the room for large-group activities such as demonstrations and exhibitions, but most of the room is subdivided into studios where teachers work on projects with small groups of students. This arrangement gives participants the flexibility to regroup, team up, or borrow tools and materials as the project requires.

Third, community representatives are invited to help create a context for students' efforts. Staff members from city agencies and programmes identify unmet community needs that students could address and also serve as an authentic audience for students' finished products and presentations.

At a recent exhibition of students' work, several teams of students displayed drawings and scale models of a heritage museum they had designed for Cambridge. Each group had a different conception of where the museum might be located and how it should be designed. The museum builders sat with their models to explain their ideas as parents, city officials and local business people filtered through the exhibit.

In making the models, the museum builders were responding to a request from the city's tourist agency, which is in the process of raising funds for a museum. Six weeks before the exhibit, the agency director had come to speak to CityWorks students and ask for their help in this effort. With thousands of people visiting the city each year, it was important for students to understand the tourism industry and to help plan its development in a way that would take the needs of residents into account.

In addition to the museum builders, several other groups of students involved themselves in the question of what visitors to the city should see and do. Rejecting existing brochures featuring 'Old Cambridge' and Harvard University, one group designed a tour and brochure featuring places of interest to visiting teenagers, while another created a 'Sweet Tour' brochure for visitors seeking the best desserts in town. A third group of students liked the idea of highlighting the efforts of a 'local hero'. They videotaped an interview with John E. Gittens, a founder of the Cambridge NAACP, and learned that he had led a neighbourhood organizing effort to get the city to open a new playground named after a child who was struck by a car when he was playing in the street. Their brochure featured a map locating the playground as well as the story of its creation. All three brochures, along with a T-shirt that another group of CityWorks students designed, have since been adopted by the board of the tourist agency as products that are marketed and distributed.

The goal of CityWorks projects is to help students understand their community and its needs, and ultimately to see themselves as people who can affect that community and create new opportunities for themselves and others who live or work there. Through the lens of community development, students arrive at a very different and more positive vision of what it means to be a vocational student. The point is not just to make things, learn some skills and get a job, but rather to become thinkers and solvers of problems who work well together in teams and communicate well with various audiences.

Towards participatory democracy in school

If Paulina had entered Rindge four years ago, the programme she entered would have been very different from CityWorks, but remarkably similar to the one in place in 1888, when Rindge opened. In fact, thousands of other high schools in this country today still offer such a programme: freshmen in vocational education go through an 'exploratory' in which they sample each of the shops available in the school, such as metalworking and carpentry. Teachers work in the autonomous isolation of their shops or classrooms; students suffer from low expectations and minimal or diluted academics.

This system, unchanged since its original design for the industrial revolution over a hundred years ago, is based on an outdated and undemocratic premise that 15-year-olds of lower income families should predict their adult occupation (Rosenstock 1991). (Who among us at 15 thought we would be doing what we are doing today?) In short, the 9th grade programme functions as the gatekeeping mechanism that begins the stark segregation of vocational students by social class, race, gender and language ability.

In choosing CityWorks, we rejected the purely consumerist notion of democracy so prevalent in American high schools today, which is that schools offering the most options in courses and shops are best – even if these offerings are shallow and force students into a track. Our goal was to move towards a more participatory model where teachers work together towards the collective interests of the students and the school; where students are engaged, active participants in their learning and in their community; and where parents and community members have real roles in the school's programmes. We saw a new mission: to use vocational methods – experiential and contextual learning, team teaching, cooperative learning and performance assessment – so that vocational students can learn the same basic and advanced academic skills and critical thinking skills that *all* students should learn for further education or for work.

In 1990, more through instinct than anything else, we began a participatory planning process to develop a new 9th grade programme. What we did not realize is that the process of creating CityWorks would be as important in developing a democratic culture as the programme itself – because of its impact on teachers.

In embarking on programme redesign, we set ourselves three ground rules. The first was to keep everyone in the department informed of all that we were doing. The second was that nobody would have to participate who did not want to. And the third was that those who did not want to participate would not be allowed to interfere with the efforts of those who did. When the first call went out for people to join a design team, six people volunteered.

Letting the teachers lead

By the autumn of 1991, the team had come up with an overall conceptual framework for CityWorks, fiddled with the schedule to create unprecedented daily meeting time for teachers, and begun to design and renovate a space that would house the new programme. We began the school year with enough classroom activities to last only about one month. The rest would have to come from the CityTeam meetings in which everyone teaching the course would participate. Although not having all of CityWorks plotted out was a bit terrifying, we knew that handing teachers a finished curriculum would be a mistake.

Teachers, like students, are not empty vessels into which the current wisdom can be poured. For years, vocational teachers at Rindge had spent virtually all of their time at school teaching occupationally specific, narrow, technical skills. Most believed this is what being a vocational teacher was all about. State-mandated curricula reinforced this notion. Vocational teachers received manuals for their shop areas listing duties and tasks that were to fill the students' days.

If we wanted our school to be a place where all kids could be active participants in a democratic culture, we would have to structure a programme where all teachers could be too. We would have to encourage teachers to unearth the reasons beneath their current practice, and to reconsider that practice in the light of changing economic and social realities. In other words, we had to respect and make room for them as thinkers as well as doers.

We suspected that Rindge teachers were experiencing a kind of cognitive dissonance. Certainly the curriculum they were teaching at school left out much of what they knew to be important in their own work and lives outside of school. This point was brought home to us early in our reform efforts during a conversation with a teacher who had taught carpentry at Rindge for many years. Like many vocational teachers, he was an independent contractor outside of school. He explained that he would very much like to turn his business over to his sons, both of whom were skilled carpenters. The problem was that neither seemed to be good at most of the other tasks associated with running a successful contracting business: for instance, making good estimates, writing contracts, managing cash flow, dealing with clients and subcontractors and getting variances from the local zoning board. These are all skills that are rarely taught in vocational schools.

This teacher held within his own experiences the seeds of a new approach to practice. The students in his classes should not be limited to banging nails, but should learn the range of skills that he knew as a parent, citizen and small contractor were needed by his own sons.[3] The challenge for us has been to create a professional culture that encourages teachers to share their experiences and reflect on their practice. Several strategies have been particularly critical to that effort.

Common planning time

The most basic change we have made is to give teachers both informal and formal opportunities to work together. Their close physical proximity in the CityWorks room opens the possibility of joint projects. Daily required CityTeam meetings ensure that such possibilities will be discussed.

To create a meeting time in the daily schedule necessitated closing the shops for a period, an unpopular move with both our own teachers and the counsellors from other parts of the high school who signed students up for shops as electives. But the daily meeting time is critical to what we are trying to accomplish. The meetings are a time to reflect on what is happening in CityWorks, to review, revise, and propose curriculum activities and, more generally, to get to know one another and explore the possibilities for collaboration.

Including 'outsiders'
From the beginning, the vocational teachers who staffed CityWorks have been joined by a variety of people from very different backgrounds who bring other perspectives and experiences to the task. The 'others' have included several academic teachers, a loaned employee from the Polaroid Corporation, bilingual technical assistants, and, as needed, consultants to assist staff – first in their work on curriculum, later on group dynamics and issues of organizational development. Teachers and students must gain experience in and understanding of the new relationships required of them by the world outside of school.

This mixture creates a forum for re-examining assumptions and for moving beyond the specific skills involved in particular trades or subjects to what is important for all students to know and be able to do by the time they leave the programme. At one critical junction, for example, when vocational teachers were resisting collaborative projects in the name of craft specialization, the Polaroid employee talked about the multicraft perspective at his company and at other high-performance workplaces.

Creating genuine interdependence
Curricular integration, an end in itself, produces important changes in teacher relationships as well. Once isolated in their

own shops, and sometimes competing among themselves for students, teachers now plan curriculum and multidisciplinary projects together. As a result, they are more invested in the whole performance of each student, as well as the performance of the whole school.

The daily teacher meetings are productive because they have to be. All teachers know they are about to go in and teach CityWorks the next day (or the next hour). In a very real sense, they sink or swim together. If the programme works, it will eventually increase enrolments and attract a broader clientele of students. If it does not, Rindge will suffer the kinds of staff cutbacks seen in other vocational programmes. The competitive ethic of the old exploratory does not die easily, but it really is counterproductive in the new structure. It makes much more sense to collaborate, to nurture and support new ideas, and to look to one another for project ideas and strategies. This shared reflection has contributed to a new level of collegiality at Rindge. Teachers more often talk with one another about teaching. They plan and make instructional materials together, they observe one another, and they are willing to ask for and provide one another with assistance.

Changing expectations

Changes are evident in both the formal team meetings and informal time that staff spend with one another. During the first few months of CityWorks team meetings, teachers would almost never comment on a teaching or learning issue without prefacing their remarks with a disclaimer: 'I would never say what's right for anyone else', or 'This is just the way I do things', or 'I know that everyone has their own way of doing things and that's fine.'

The frequency of such statements provided clues to an underlying group norm that can best be characterized as 'non-interference': 'I won't look too closely at what you're up to or tell you what to do; and you won't scrutinize me' (Little 1992, p. 49). The isolation of traditional schools and the conditions of teaching make teachers view their work with the sometimes fierce independence of artisans (Huberman 1989). For vocational teachers, this perspective is reinforced by their highly special-ized work within the school (and outside) as trade artisans.

In the past, Rindge teachers defended the separateness of their shops by citing the differences among their trades, each with its own specific skill requirements. Shop autonomy seemed a natural, and even necessary, condition of vocational educa-tion. The most obvious negative side-effect was the competition for students. But perhaps an even more serious problem was that teachers had no reason to identify, nor any real way to address, the broader educational needs of their students. They focused on finding ways to interest students in specific tech-nical areas, but they did not feel responsible for ensuring that all students become better problem solvers or communicators, or gain a solid base of reading, writing and quantitative and scientific reasoning skills.

It is impossible to pin-point a moment when the focus changed, but after two years of team meetings, a sense of broader responsibility is now evident within the group. Teachers now share information and are willing to identify competencies that students need regardless of their schooling or career choices. Staff members routinely team up for multicraft projects, and they sometimes even design classroom projects that do not involve their trade specialty at all.

In the early planning stages for CityWorks, the group tended to swing from cynical scepticism ('This will never work!') to unrealistic enthusiasm ('We're almost done!'). Now teachers approach the task of restructuring with a kind of rolling up of the collective sleeves. We all have a noticeably greater toler-ance for ambiguity. People are more willing to bring issues to the team for group problem solving and have found ways to deal constructively with disagreements.

Teachers are also evolving a shared language for talking about how they work together and for getting through the inevitable crises. Perhaps more important, we now have a picture of what we could and should become: a high-performance workplace where staff members are highly interdependent, yet each is an active participant, focusing energy on the tasks at hand.

The amount of time devoted to meetings and the intensity of the staff work have, at times, created a worry that we might become too adult-focused. A school committee member once railed, 'I'm sick and tired of hearing about how happy the teachers are at Rindge. What about the kids?' Fortunately, students do not seem to feel this way. When new students are asked what is most noticeable or important to them about Rindge, most begin with this simple statement: 'The teachers here really care about you'.

Of course, the teachers have always cared about students, but the scope of what they care about has broadened considerably and hence is more evident to the students. In the old way of doing business, teachers had little patience with students who were not ready to make a choice about what they wanted to be and who were not motivated to learn all of the skills of a particular trade. They felt their identity as skilled craftspeople slipping away, to be replaced by a much less desirable identity as 'caretakers of marginal students' (Little 1992, p. 26).

CityWorks and the other integrated programmes give teachers a new identity. Even if students do not express interest in particular trades, teachers no longer feel like mere caretakers. They know that they can help students develop competencies, interests, and attitudes that will serve them well in future schooling or work. Teachers' feelings of self-efficacy are evident to students. Several first year students recently surprised a visiting reporter by telling her that what makes Rindge teachers different is that they *like* what they are doing.

Not surprisingly, students respond by becoming more engaged with school; their 'creative juices' get going and teachers get to see them at their best. The caring and mutual respect go beyond the classroom walls. For example, during the summer a group of students who had just completed their CityWorks year responded to the invitation from one of their teachers to come up with ways to smooth the entry of incoming new students. Using the abbreviation RSTA (from the Rindge School of Technical Arts), they named themselves 'Responsible Students Take Action'.

When Paulina and her cohort entered Rindge, they received a new student handbook, covering all of the things the older students wished someone had told them, and they found immediate support in the form of RSTA student mentors, who had set up a table in the hall to help with everything from coping with sticky locks on lockers to dealing with harassment from older students.

Impressed by such efforts, staff members have become willing to carve out even more unusual forums for student participation and input. Rindge is probably the only vocational school in America to have its own Innovations Board, with equal membership (and votes) for students and staff. The board was created in late 1991, soon after CityWorks received an Innovations Award from the Ford Foundation. One of ten innovations in state and local government selected nationally from over 1700 applicants, CityWorks was given $100,000 to 'broaden and deepen' the work.

The staff agreed to set aside one-third of this award to be distributed over three years in small grants to other innovations in the Cambridge Schools that would further the CityWorks mission. The process would be overseen by a board with equal representation of students and staff and several slots reserved for community representatives.

At its first few meetings, the board hammered out a mission statement and a set of priorities. Student members were outspoken in these discussions, insisting, for example, that all proposals be submitted by at least one teacher and one student, and that proposals specify the ways in which students would be involved in carrying out the programme.

By the spring, board members were reading and evaluating nearly two dozen proposals from all over the school district. After selecting and interviewing the finalists, the board selected nine winners, with proposals ranging from a new student-run radio programme to a special summer school for bilingual students. Questioned by teachers and classmates as to why they did not use more of the money internally for Rindge projects and programmes, several students spoke passionately of the need to end the isolation of the vocational programme. They want the Innovations Fund to encourage teachers and students throughout the school district to try new ways to join hands and minds. Their hope echoes the note sounded by Paulina at the end of her statement to the school: 'We give respect, so we expect respect. Success demands it!'

Bringing change out in the open

Educators involved in school reform efforts tend to build a protective wall around what they are doing. If they do not, they believe, they might be accused by parents – or even worse, by school board members – of 'experimenting with our children'. Although it is possible to work in isolation for a while, the only real protection in the long run lies in convincing key stakeholders of the value, and perhaps the inevitability, of what you are doing.

The changes at Rindge have never been a secret. Staff members and students have made presentations at Parents' Nights, spoken at each of the junior high schools, and hosted hundreds of people at the exhibitions of student work. The interest in CityWorks expressed by the larger community has motivated the staff to make the new programme work well and to be able to describe it well to others.

The publicness of what we are doing has caused some local political problems. Speaking for a small but vocal constituency of parents, one school board member accused Rindge of misdirecting working-class students by offering them liberal arts rather than the manual training that they 'need'. This attack was made through letters to the editor of the local paper, obstruction of even mundane Rindge matters before the school committee, and encouragement of students to leave the district under a state school-choice plan and attend a suburban vocational school. There were requests for state audits in three consecutive years, and one even included an attempt to get the state to decertify our programme.

Thus far, such attacks have taken time and energy, but they have also solidified the staff, students and parents behind the new programme. Fortunately, we also receive very positive feedback about what we are doing, both from within the district and around the country. As awareness of the Perkins Act has grown, so have requests to visit our programme or to send our teachers out as workshop leaders and presenters. In fact, the requests eventually became so great that we set up our own formal mechanism for handling them: the Hands and Minds Collaborative, funded by the Dewitt Wallace–Readers Digest Foundation and the Mott Foundation, is a joint effort of Rindge and the Center for Law and Education.

Contact with other teachers and other school systems has brought major benefits to our staff. The attitudes, questions, and comments of teachers from other districts become a yardstick against which Rindge teachers can measure the distance they have come, and can reduce the 'general physical, social, and educational separation that divorces vocational teachers' from other practitioners (Little 1992, p. 6).

In June 1993, a dozen Rindge teachers served as workshop leaders at a national conference co-sponsored by the Center for Law and Education, the Massachusetts Institute of Technology, and the Hands and Minds Collaborative. It was the job of the workshop leaders to assist the nearly two hundred participants in developing projects that would help them implement the Perkins Act in their own schools. At the last session, after listening to a number of teachers express concerns about the loss of time for trade-specific training, Tom Lividoti, the electrical teacher at Rindge, spoke up: 'I used to sound just like that. I was the loudest one complaining about fewer hours in the electrical shop. But what we're doing now brings out creative juices I didn't know kids had; I see developments on the academic end that I never dreamed were possible. I may not be able to turn out second-year apprentice electricians, but I know we are turning out better all-around students.'

Academic teachers working with the CityWorks programme have also found that they have important messages to share with their colleagues. In spring 1993, Alif Muhammad, the CitySystems teacher, convened a workshop series for Cambridge teachers called 'Put the Action Back into Maths and Science'. Rob Riordan, a member of the Rindge Humanities team, addressed humanities teachers and scholars recently at a national meeting sponsored by the American Council of Learned Societies: 'I started the year thinking it was my mission to bring humanities into vocational education. Now I believe we must bring vocational methodologies into the humanities.'

Dilemmas and challenges remain

When we began to recreate ourselves, we knew that we wanted the school to be democratic in all of its many layers. The relations between administration and staff would be as egalitarian as possible and teachers would enjoy meaningful participation in decision making. The relations between teachers would be democratic: there would be opportunities for teachers to diversify their roles, to team teach and to have regular common planning time. The relations between teachers and students would be democratic: the teacher would act as coach and adviser rather than as a distant lecturer.

The methodology and curriculum would be democratic: we would not track, and therefore we would have the same high expectations for all students. We would focus our assessment on student-originated projects, not teacher-designed tests. The relations between the school and the community would be democratic: it would afford opportunities for students to investigate and actively seek to meet real community needs. Finally, we would also try to make our physical environment – our work spaces – as democratic as possible: we would design and build spaces that further our democratic goals, despite the typical American high school architecture, which reflects the industrial factory model and 'gets in the way' of collective work.[4]

The fundamental conundrum of vocational education remains, however, insufficiently resolved: many still want from vocational education the 'no-frills' schooling that they view as suitable for lower income students, while others of us agree with Dewey that it is a vehicle for transforming secondary education and creating schools where all students can be 'smart'.

One of the most troubling aspects of our experience at Rindge is the persistent social-class bias that pervades certain community members' beliefs about who should attend vocational programmes and what they should be doing once they are there. One critic noted that the new Rindge is preparing 'Renaissance people, not plumbers'. It goes without saying which he preferred for his own daughters, yet he still insisted narrow skills were better for low-income students.

This bias has its roots in the contradictory origins of our school, and it will not fall easily in Cambridge – or elsewhere. Even Dewey, in commenting on this bias, noted with an aggravated sarcasm, 'Nothing in the history of education is more touching than to hear some successful leaders denounce as undemocratic the attempt to give all the children at public expense the fuller education which their own children enjoy as a matter of course' (Westbrook 1991, p. 178). At its core, this is what the experiment at Rindge seeks to achieve: to counter the reduction of education to job training (Davis *et al.* 1989, p. 109) that only 'erects more barriers to high-quality education for low-income students' (Rosenstock 1992), and to broaden creative intellectual work for all students.

Notes

1 The Center for Law and Education, based in Cambridge, Massachusetts, and Washington, DC, advocates for the educational rights of low-income students and parents throughout the United States of America. Paul Weckstein, co-director of the Center, was a pivotal conceptualist and advocate for the new directions called for in the Perkins Act.

2 The Perkins Act mandates that all vocational students 'gain strong experience in and understanding of all aspects of the industry they are preparing to enter, including finance, planning, management, underlying principles of technology, technical and production skills, labor issues, community issues, health and safety issues, and environmental issues as they pertain to the industry.'

3 'What the best and wisest parent wants for his own child, that must the community want for all of its children.' From J. Dewey (1990) *The School and Society*, p. 7. Chicago: University of Chicago Press.

4 Assembly line architecture is supported by assembly line methodologies and curricula. See A. Steinberg (1993) Beyond the assembly line, *The Harvard Education Letter* 9(2): 1.

References

Carnoy, M. and Levin, H. (1985) *Schooling and Work in the Democratic State*. Stanford, CA: Stanford University Press.

Davis, J., Huot, J., Jackson, N., Johnston, R., Little, D., Martell, G., Moss, P., Noble, D., Turk, J. and Wilson, G. (1989) *It's Our Own Knowledge*. Toronto: Ontario Federation of Labor Conference on Education and Training.

Dewey, J. (1993) Some dangers in the present movement for industrial education, in J. Boydston (ed.) *The Middle Works: 1899–1924*. Carbondale: Southern Illinois University Press.

Huberman, M. (1989) The model of the independent artisan in teachers' professional development, in J.W. Little and M.W. McLaughlin (eds), *Teachers' Work: Individuals, Colleagues, and Contexts*. New York: Teachers College Press.

Krug, E. (1969) *The Shaping of the American High School, 1880–1920*. Madison: University of Wisconsin Press.

Little, J.W. (1992) *Work on the Margins: The Experience of Vocational Teachers in Comprehensive High Schools*. Berkeley: National Center for Research in Vocational Education.

National Assessment of Vocational Education (1987) Washington, DC: United States Department of Education.

Rosenstock, L. (1991) The walls come down: the overdue reunification of vocational and academic education. *Phi Delta Kappan* 72(6): 434–6.

Rosenstock, L. (1992) Easing students' pressure to predict the future [Letter to the editor]. *New York Times*, 10 December, p. 20.

Westbrook, R. (1991) *John Dewey and American Democracy*. Ithaca, NY: Cornell University Press.

4 **BOB PETERSON**

La Escuela Fratney: A journey towards democracy

Editors' introduction

Advocates of democratic schools have long held that meaningful and lasting projects are most often created from the 'bottom-up' through collaboration among educators, parents and other citizens at the local school level. In this chapter, Bob Peterson, a fifth grade (10- and 11-year-olds) teacher, describes how – despite objections and obstacles from central administrative authorities – a group of progressive teachers and parents created a two-way bilingual elementary school in Milwaukee, Wisconsin. Although the school is especially noted for its bilingual programme, its multicultural and antiracist curriculum and its collaborative governance, it also employs such progressive methods as whole language literacy instruction, cooperative learning and the use of a problem-based thematic curriculum. Several of the faculty, including Peterson, are also widely known for their involvement in Rethinking Schools, a progressive education collaborative that sponsors a nationally distributed quarterly newspaper of the same name.

It was to have been a fairly typical student role play followed by group discussion, an activity in which students were used to participating. But, as often happens, my 5th grade students surprised me. As Gilberto, Juan and Carlos took the stage, I knew only that they would be dramatizing some form of discrimination, the topic of today's lesson. The other students and I were astounded when we realized that Gilberto and Juan were acting the part of two gay men trying to rent an apartment from Carlos, the landlord who refused to rent to them.

I was surprised in part because in previous brainstorming sessions on discrimination, nobody had mentioned discrimination against homosexuals. Further, my students had already shown they were apt to uncritically accept anti-gay slurs and stereotypes. But here were Gilberto, Juan and Carlos, on their own initiative, transferring our discussion of discrimination based on race to discrimination based on sexual preference.

The role play caused an initial chorus of laughs and catcalls, but students then listened attentively to the presentation. Afterwards, I asked the class what type of discrimination had been modelled.

'Gayism!' one student yelled out.

It was a new word, but it got the point across. The class went on to discuss 'gayism'. Most of the children who spoke agreed that it was a form of discrimination. During the discussion, one student mentioned a march on Washington a week earlier that people had organized to demand gay rights (Gilberto, Juan and Carlos said they were unaware of the march).

Elvis, who coined the term gayism, then said: 'Yeah, my cousin is one of those lesi . . . lesi . . .'

'Lesbians', I said, completing his sentence.

'Yeah, lesbians', he said. He then added enthusiastically, 'And she went to Washington to march for her rights.'

'That's just like when Dr King made his dream speech at the march in Washington', another student added.

Before long, the class moved on to a new role play, but the dramatization lingered in my memory. I was proud that the class had been able to move beyond our typical discussions of gay issues, which had seemed to centre on my explaining why

students should not call each other 'faggot'. More fundamentally, however, the incident reminded me of the inherent links
between classroom and society: how society influences the
children who show up in our classrooms for six hours a day
and how broader movements for social reform affect daily
classroom life.

Some might think it unusual for 5th grade students to dramat-
ize discrimination against homosexuals. But then, many things
about La Escuela Fratney may surprise those used to more traditional forms of schooling.

The struggle to establish La Escuela Fratney

Forged in a battle with a recalcitrant school administration,
La Escuela Fratney in Milwaukee, Wisconsin, is the site of a
continuing journey to create a school governed by parents
and teachers. We describe ourselves as a two-way bilingual,
multicultural, whole language school governed by a site-based
council. The school currently has 360 students in 4-year-old
kindergarten to 5th grade, of whom 65 per cent are Hispanic;
20 per cent, African American; 13 per cent, white; and the
remainder, Asian and Native American. Nearly 70 per cent of
students are eligible for free lunches. We have a Learning Disabilities programme conducted primarily through team teaching, and we have a separate programme for 3–5-year-olds with
exceptional needs.

At each new leg of our journey, we have encountered significant problems that reflect how our society, despite its
democratic rhetoric, is in many ways undemocratic. Among
the problems: a central office wedded to autocratic methods of
leadership, a school system structured to inhibit collaborative
teaching practices, parents and teachers tied to the authoritarian
habits of their own schooling, students conditioned by a mass-
media culture that values individual consumption over the
common good, and a socioeconomic system that places little
value on urban schools and the families served by them.

In this chapter, you will learn how a group of committed
teachers and parents dealt with these problems. You will find out

how the school attempts to meaningfully involve all parents, not just the most educated and articulate, in the work of the school. Also, you will see how the school attempts to uphold its democratic ideals, despite pressures ranging from budget cuts to drugs and violence.

Political battles

The 90-year-old Fratney Street School was marked for demolition. In April 1988, the staff and students of the school were to move to a new building six blocks away. That the neighbourhood around Fratney was one of the few racially integrated, working-class neighbourhoods in the city meant little to the school bureaucracy. Some people, however, had a vision of Fratney as the home of an educational programme that capitalized on the unique features of the neighbourhood. As one parent said, 'We started to dream about a school that would provide the highest quality education for all of our children, black, white and Hispanic'.

On 1 January 1988, this small group of teachers, parents and community activists made their vision public by issuing a press release under the name Neighbors for a New Fratney. The press release called on the Milwaukee School Board to support our proposal to create a whole language, two-way bilingual, multicultural site-based-managed school at the Fratney School site. We called this new school La Escuela Fratney.

School administrators, however, wanted to turn the building into a new school, an Exemplary Teaching Center staffed by master teachers using the techniques of Madeline Hunter.[1] District teachers having classroom difficulties would then come to the center for $2\frac{1}{2}$-week training sessions, working with 'master' teachers in their classrooms. Many parents questioned whether kids should be taught by a series of bad teachers. They also argued that a teaching centre could be established anywhere, while the success of La Escuela Fratney depended on its being in one of the few multiracial neighbourhoods in Milwaukee.

Neighbors for a New Fratney (NNF) held community meetings and mobilized for a key public hearing. The hearing coincided with a bitter snowstorm that forced all schools to close the next day. Still, the turnout for the meeting was so large that it convinced school board members of the need to give NNF's proposal serious consideration. They directed school administrators to meet with our group and come back with a revised recommendation.

From the beginning, the leaders at the central office did not appear to understand NNF's proposal. Although they issued a compromise proposal that they said combined their teacher training programme with our project, many features of our proposal were the antithesis of theirs. For example, a central point of our proposal was that the school would be run by a site-based council of parents and teachers; the administrators wanted a teacher training school organized and run by the central office. As we negotiated with the top administrators in the superintendent's conference room, the absurdity of the situation became evident. I pointed out to then-superintendent Hawthorne Faison that there was an inherent contradiction between a school run by a staff development academy and a school run by a local group of teachers and parents. The central office's proposal for the Exemplary Teacher Center did not even mention parents.

'Wait!' responded one top administrative official. 'While it's true we didn't mention parents once in our proposal, your proposal didn't mention central office.'

We stuck to our position and continued to mobilize the community. Several developments gave us additional momentum. A few months earlier, the school board had publicly gone on record in favour of site-based management. School board members had also become aware of the benefits of a whole language teaching approach, in part due to the efforts of *Rethinking Schools*, a quarterly newspaper published in Milwaukee whose editorial board included two members of NNF (Peterson 1987, 1988; Tenorio 1986, 1988). In addition, members of the African American community, led by Howard Fuller (our current superintendent), were demanding an independent school district, charging among other things that the bureaucracy was incapable of listening to African American parents.

The long and short of it was that the school board passed the proposal and established the first citywide specialty school to give enrolment preference to children living in the school's immediate neighbourhood. The board also directed the central office to cooperate with NNF.

One additional factor seemed to enter into the board's decision, at least for one member. A few months after the vote, this member confessed to me that his approval of La Escuela Fratney was strongly influenced by the quality of the teaching his son was receiving in the 1st grade classroom of a whole language teacher. During a key school board meeting, he said, he found himself during a break discussing the Fratney proposal with a top administrator and realized that the man did not have the slightest idea of what the proposal involved. 'Quite honestly', the board member told me, 'I didn't really know what you were talking about either, but I knew this much: My son had started 1st grade in the classroom of a teacher who used what she called whole language techniques. By Thanksgiving, my kid was coming home and writing and publishing his own books, excited about reading and writing, loving to read and to be read to. I knew I had to support your proposal.'

The school board's approval essentially concluded the first stage of our struggle, the struggle for political power. It had lasted eight weeks.

Administrative battles

During the second stage, we confronted the basic tasks involved in developing the programme: renovating the facility, selecting the principal and other staff, putting in place the curriculum and related materials. Unfortunately, what the administration failed to do politically at the board level, they tried to do administratively.

For example, despite the school board's explicit order that the central office should cooperate with NNF, two weeks passed with no meeting or contact between the two groups. Finally, we heard through a friend at central office that an important meeting to plan the new Fratney was to take place the next day, a Friday, at 11.00 am. Uninvited, NNF members asked a parent to attend. Because the parent had no idea where the meeting was to be held, she waited five minutes after the meeting was scheduled to begin, and then approached the secretary of the administrator in charge and asked to be taken to the meeting. The secretary, who did not know this parent had not been invited, escorted her into a room of open-mouthed administrators. At that time, a joint meeting was set up to start the planning.

For the next several months, from March to September, administrators placed one obstacle after another in the way of constructing the new programme. We also had to contend with the typical bureaucratic procedures of a 100,000-student school system, which were not designed to effectively support any sort of grass-roots initiative. These problems were compounded because few members of NNF had the time or expertise to navigate the administrative bureaucracy; most of our volunteers worked on the Fratney project after putting in a full day of work. Our recommendations were often ignored or approved only late in the process.

For example, to deal with union seniority rules that might allow teachers to transfer to Fratney even though they disagreed with the programme's approach, NNF proposed that announcements of staff openings be accompanied by a one-page explanation of the school's programme. The Milwaukee Teachers Education Association agreed, as did lower level administrators. But the higher authorities decided against this strategy.

NNF called for a nationwide search for a principal. The administration refused, and then proceeded to stall in hiring anyone. Finally, a month before school was to open, and in opposition to what a parent committee had recommended, the administration recommended the appointment of a woman whose experience was limited to suburban schools. She was bilingual, but in English and German, not English and Spanish. NNF viewed this action as a direct affront to the community, and once again the community mobilized. Dozens of parents came to school board meetings, many of them waving picket signs.

Bowing to pressure and publicity, newly hired Superintendent Robert S. Peterkin (from Cambridge, Massachusetts) recognized the problem and rejected the recommendation. Peterkin hired an interim principal acceptable to the community.

Developing the curriculum posed additional problems. In late June and July, three teachers settled in at the central office building to write a draft curriculum. Resources for the teachers seemed almost non-existent: The teachers were given information only in response to specific questions, and secretarial help seemed in extremely short supply. One of the teachers remarked that working on the Fratney project at the central office was like being a peace activist in the Pentagon.

The stonewalling continued. For example, despite repeated requests, the administrator in charge of ordering furniture refused to exchange the school's old 'bicycle desks' (chairs attached to desks) for separate desks and chairs, which are more conducive to cooperative grouping. One day, a member of NNF told the administrator that we had changed our minds: We wanted the old desks to stay because on the first day of school, parents, teachers and students were going to pile them on the playground and then call a press conference to expose the administration for failing to support our project. The next morning, two lorry-loads of new desks were delivered to the school.

When the new staff arrived in mid-August to make what we thought were to be final preparations for an opening a few weeks later, we found that necessary renovation had only begun and that the school had not been cleaned since the spring. Curiously, nothing we had ordered in July had yet arrived. We called the suppliers and they told us they had no record of our orders. Much to our horror, we discovered that although the requisition forms had been signed on July 18th or earlier by an associate superintendent, the forms had sat in the purchasing division for a month because the department did not have an authorization card with the associate superintendent's signature. The missing materials were a serious problem; many books had disappeared when the school closed, the two-way bilingual programme required new materials and the few remaining library books were in boxes because of the delayed renovation of the library. We would have to start school with virtually no materials. 'Well, at least we ordered a high-quality Xerox machine', one teacher said hopefully. 'We can rely on that for the first few weeks of school.' But, of course, a phone call confirmed that this order, too, had somehow been lost.

We stormed into the central office building. Fortunately, this time we had two allies: Superintendent Peterkin and his assistant, Deborah McGriff, who was flabbergasted by our story. She listened intently as we hinted that our next step would be a round-the-clock occupation of the school. She took immediate steps to get the administrators in line. A photocopy machine appeared in the school the next day. Materials were shipped via airmail. At a meeting the next day, the administrators who had put up road blocks were now at our beck and call.

After visiting La Escuela Fratney on the first day of school, Superintendent Peterkin called Fratney a model of his version of school reform, referring specifically to the value of extensive parental involvement and a unified vision of what a school should be. Finally, the tide had turned.

Implementation battles

Now that La Escuela Fratney had actually opened, we thought we could finally direct our energies and attention to the business of implementing the new programme. Unfortunately, the consequences of the months of forced inaction and poor planning were acutely felt throughout the first year. The time we had to plan the school was too short to begin with and the low-level combat the administration's opposition had generated diverted our attention to matters that should not have been a problem. But such conflicts had a positive effect too. They brought parents and teachers together and taught us that a successful urban school needs an active parent/teacher/community alliance to sustain it and a common vision of what the school is working towards. Our ability to overcome these problems also gave us the courage and energy to confront the many challenges that lay ahead.

Key components of the Fratney programme

Starting a new school with several important components was an immense challenge, even with the high level of energy coming off the successful struggle to establish the school. In theory, the components fit well together, but in daily classroom life, each took a big effort to get going well. We consider each to be an integral part of our school's vision.

Two-way bilingual programme

An important component of the Fratney programme is our commitment to a two-way bilingual programme in which native Spanish and English speakers are in the same classrooms, with children receiving half their instruction in English and half in Spanish. This arrangement avoids separating children by language dominance and gives meaning and purpose to the acquisition of two languages.

The belief anchoring this approach is that all children have the right to learn two languages, including their native language. By consciously striving to create equality between the languages in our building, we are modelling a broad concept of equality for our children. Given the intimate link between culture and language, instruction in two languages also promotes multicultural understanding. Additionally, a two-way bilingual approach enhances students' self-esteem, because students soon learn that no matter what social class they come from, they bring something of value to the classroom: their language.

Two-way bilingual programmes in the United States of America, however, have numerous problems (Edelsky 1991), primarily stemming from the politically subordinate role any second language necessarily has in this country. Fratney's programme is no exception. We have learned that successful bilingual learning requires a strict separation of the two languages and language environments, so children are forced to use their second language and teachers are encouraged to stay in the target language. If classes are always conducted bilingually (that is, a teacher explains the material first in one language and then another), students may rely on their native tongue.

By the end of our second year, we realized that English was still too dominant in our school. We looked at the experience of two-way bilingual schools in other cities and critically examined our practices. Discussions were held among staff, at a site-based council meeting, and at a special meeting of parents of students in the two kindergarten classrooms where the method for bilingual instruction differed from that used in the rest of the school. At the beginning of our third year, we adopted for the whole school the instructional method used in these kindergartens: Two teachers of the same grade team-teach between 54 and 60 children in two groups of 27–30 children per class. One day, they go to the Spanish room and receive instruction in Spanish; the next day, they go to the English room and receive instruction in English. The teachers are bilingual, but one teaches in English and one in Spanish. This approach has increased the use of Spanish in our school and encouraged team teaching. At the same time, it has exacerbated the problem of lack of common planning time and complicated other matters such as assessment, report cards and parent–teacher conferences. In our seventh year of operation, the 4th and 5th grade teachers addressed these problems by alternating classes every two calendar weeks instead of every other day. This arrangement allows for more consistent instruction and more timely completion of student projects.

Although Fratney's programme has clearly been successful in helping students with limited English proficiency learn English while maintaining their Spanish, it has been less successful in helping native English speakers learn Spanish. The staff and parents are trying to address this problem through peer observation, research of other schools that may be more successful and a comparative analysis of the English-dominant students who excel in the programme and those who do not.

Despite these problems, the two-way bilingual programme is one of Fratney's strengths. It sends a strong message to students and their families about the equivalent value of Spanish and English and the people who speak these languages. Because

Spanish-speaking parents know the school values their language, they feel more comfortable in visiting and volunteering at our school. The bilingual programme has sent a signal to the larger Latino community that staff and parents of La Escuela Fratney are strongly committed to broader issues of equality.

Multicultural, antiracist curriculum

Our vision of multiculturalism goes beyond what we call 'the three F's': facts, foods, and faces. Although our classes include projects that focus on human relations, they also include lessons on race and power. We highlight the experiences of people of colour in our schoolwide themes, and we attempt to draw on music, history, art, stories, poetry and literature from various geopolitical groups, such as African Americans, Hispanics, Native Americans and Asian Americans. We also teach our students to be antiracist; we teach that racism is unscientific and immoral, that it has been a damaging social disease throughout US history. Teachers are encouraged to teach about stereotypes, prejudice and all forms of discrimination.

Given the diversity of our student and family population, such a multicultural, antiracist policy is important not only for our long-range educational goals but also for our immediate survival as a community of learners.

The success of this curriculum has been uneven. Some of the more outspoken white, middle-class parents complained that our school was teaching only minority history and short-changing students of European heritage. Others complained that their kids were not learning the national anthem and the pledge of allegiance. Some teachers felt that such criticism, if left unchecked, would push Fratney back into the mainstream, where curricular content might talk of democracy, but violate what many consider one of the fundamental building blocks of democracy – the equality of all people – in its continued emphasis on European points of view.

At times, such issues exploded at meetings. For example, at one site-based council meeting, a white parent questioned the absence of the pledge of allegiance in the classroom, and a young Puerto Rican teacher responded by describing how angry she became every time she had to recite the pledge of allegiance, because it reminded her that Puerto Rico has endured decades of US colonial rule without 'liberty and justice for all'. The parent said she had never realized anyone at the school might have felt that way.

Such differences of opinion do not go away and the absence of such controversy at a school does not mean differences do not exist; it is more likely that people are just mirroring our society's propensity to remain silent on the sensitive issue of race. A school that wants to foster a healthy multicultural atmosphere should be committed to sustaining an ongoing conversation about matters of race and culture in such a way that all voices are present and dominant modes of thought are challenged.

One of Fratney's strategies for encouraging the expression of diverse points of view was to develop a year-long process in which the staff and parents defined what we meant by multicultural, antiracist education. Working through the parent curriculum committee, the site-based management council and staff meetings, parents and staff went through five drafts to come up with a joint statement that outlines the philosophy and implementation of multicultural, antiracist education at La Escuela Fratney.

The statement is a good starting point, and helps orient new staff and parents, but no document can capture the learning process that was the year-long debate itself. Thus, we have sought to find additional ways to sustain the conversation and increase our understanding of how to teach multiculturally.

We have also found it useful to define multicultural, antiracist education on a continuum, as described by educators James Banks (1991) and Enid Lee (Miner 1991). Such a framework is helpful in giving teachers a reasonable way to view their growth in this area. The continuum begins with teachers just talking about the contributions of people of colour, then adding material to the existing curriculum. It moves to thoroughly integrating instruction on non-European cultures into many subject areas. Finally, it develops to a more transformative and active stage where students and teachers critique the messages they get from television, children's books, and textbooks. The ultimate goal is that students and teachers not only understand the world, but engage in social action to change it.

Even with the school policy statement and the continuum, we discovered some problems. First, there were unnecessary duplications and omissions in what was covered. For example, a student going from kindergarten to 5th grade studied little Asian American history and too much African American history focused on Harriet Tubman and Martin Luther King Jr. Second, as new staff came to the school, they needed more specificity than either the policy statement or continuum provided.

Using another process that involved staff inservice and discussions at site-based management meetings, we came up with a document that lays out a framework for which geopolitical groups should (at a minimum) be emphasized at which grade level, thus ensuring that students are exposed to the history and culture of each major group at least twice during their years at Fratney.

Whole language and natural second language learning

We believe children learn to listen, speak, read and write by listening, speaking, reading and writing. Our classrooms aim to be student-centred, experience-based and language-rich. What does this mean? All of our students write in journals daily. We use big books, shared reading, book clubs, story telling, the writing process, interactive journals, drama and puppetry. Many classrooms publish books written by our students, and the books are then catalogued and shelved in our school library.

A fundamental reason for this approach to language arts instruction is our belief that education should be based on the experience of the children, and be relevant to their lives, families and communities. By thinking, investigating and writing about our community, children reconfirm their own and their families' worth, and simultaneously gain knowledge about the problems that they and our society as a whole must confront. Many teachers use homework assignments that encourage children to survey their community and interview family members and neighbours. This activity validates the importance of what the average person thinks and also forges stronger ties between family, school and community.

Our approach to language arts instruction has led to considerable debate and discussion in the Fratney community. Even though parents must volunteer to send their children to Fratney, many do so unaware of the school's particular instructional philosophy, which occasionally creates problems. Some parents find the teaching methods foreign because they are unlike those they experienced. Others are critical because they fear that when their kids enter the real world they will have to be familiar with textbooks, spelling tests and standardized tests.

The issue of how to teach spelling has perhaps occupied as much time at our curricular meetings as any other topic. There has been no easy way to resolve the conflicting opinions on this subject, basically because there is no surefire way to teach spelling. We have conducted numerous workshops and discussions on spelling and whole language, stressing that the key to successful language learning is involvement in meaningful reading and writing experiences. At the same time, we cannot escape the political pressures that come with the annual publishing of test scores in the local paper and have adapted to these by ensuring that we teach test-taking skills as a life-survival skill.

Cooperative learning and discipline

Cooperative learning and classroom management come up in almost any discussion of democracy in schools. The first year of the Fratney programme verged on disaster because we overestimated the responsibilities our students would be able to handle. Specifically, we failed to anticipate that a large percentage of the children who chose to come to our school were having little success at their previous school. Many students lacked basic self-management skills. They were unable to handle rights as simple as being able to take a pass and go to the bathroom on their own (that is, without direct teacher permission).

We realized that we had to consciously help students make the transition from the past, where they had been treated like mindless sheep, to the future, where we wanted them to act like responsible human beings.

During our second year, we wrote a Chapter I proposal that put a self-esteem specialist in our school full-time.[2] She team-taught with classroom teachers, using specific interventions to enhance students' self-esteem. We also built a peer mediation programme involving our 4th and 5th grade students, which has met with moderate success. We do considerable cross-age tutoring, with older children helping the younger ones as they read and write books together. This kind of tutoring helps both groups of students. For example, a 4th grade teacher was having trouble with her students' behaviour when they went on walking field trips to the nearby Milwaukee River. The children would get too close to certain parts of the river. This behaviour changed dramatically when she paired her students with 1st grade students. The older students outdid themselves to make sure that the younger students did not go too near the water.

Our teachers also use class meetings, not only to help set classroom rules at the beginning of each year but to solve problems throughout the year, and to plan each class's approach to our schoolwide themes.

Many of our teachers use a cooperative management approach that involves dividing the class into groups. For example, I arrange the desks in my classroom in five groups of six desks, each of which is a base group. Every group has its own bookshelf where materials are stored and homework is turned in. Each group elects a captain, who makes sure materials are in order and group members are paying attention and participating in activities.

I divide students into mixed groups every nine weeks, taking into account language dominance, race, gender and special needs. Throughout the day, students may work in a variety of other cooperative learning configurations, but their base group remains the same. The base group arrangement allows students to take on many of the classroom management tasks, which helps them develop a sense of responsibility for the functioning of the class. This arrangement also provides positive peer pressure that helps kids work better in the classroom.

None the less, discipline problems persist, sometimes chronic ones. These kinds of problems require both long-term curricular planning, such as teaching children 'I messages' and setting up peer mediation programmes, and short-term intervention strategies. Our culture does a great job of teaching children to be disrespectful of people on the basis of a host of attributes. While our multicultural curriculum addresses this problem throughout students' years at Fratney, teachers must act decisively to improve students' immediate behaviour. Maggie Melvin, the school librarian, talked about how teachers deal with disruptions and put-downs when she told *Teaching Tolerance* magazine that 'So often, when we're in the middle of an incident, we want to fix-it, make everything OK, and go on with the lesson. But here [at Fratney], we try to make sure that when you're in the middle of the incident, it gets processed. . . . Those are the truly teachable moments in terms of human relations, and if you believe that's an important lifetime skill, you stop the lesson and deal with it' (Ahlgren 1993, p. 30).

A thematic curriculum approach

We try to integrate as much of the curriculum as possible through schoolwide themes, which teachers and parents develop annually. Our themes generally stress social responsibility and action, as these examples illustrate: 'We respect ourselves and the world', 'We send messages when we communicate', 'We can make a difference on planet Earth' and 'We tell stories of the world'. Within the context of each theme, we also try to choose a schoolwide project. For example, in exploring the theme 'We send messages when we communicate', students studied the subtheme 'TV can be dangerous to your health'. We organized a 'no-TV week' during which students, their families and staff pledged not to watch television for an entire week.

During the theme 'We can make a difference on planet Earth', each class chose a project that they thought would show they could make a difference. The nine-week theme culminated in a project show that allowed students to share what they had done. Projects included recycling, raising money for homeless children in El Salvador, treating one another better in the classroom and testifying at a public hearing in favour of creating a nature reserve adjacent to the Milwaukee River.

Our use of schoolwide themes has helped teachers new to Fratney more quickly understand some of our underlying philosophies and methods. It has also helped bring students and staff together to work on projects, underscoring those things that we have in common.

Critical thinking

In a society whose mass culture exhibits numerous antidemocratic tendencies ranging from political apathy to institutionalized racist and sexist practices, engendering democratic sentiments within children is a challenge. At Fratney, we have a commitment to encouraging children to think deeply about the world and to helping them develop their ability to critique society and their role within it.

The 'no-TV week' project mentioned earlier is one of our strategies for raising such issues. The first year we conducted this campaign, about half the students, parents and teachers pledged not to watch any television for a week. In discussions following that week without television, the parent curriculum committee and the site-based management council met to discuss the experiment. They concluded that although not watching TV for a week might help some students permanently alter their viewing habits, the school really needed to consider how to teach children to view media critically, because the reality is that most children will continue to watch a great deal of television.

Recognizing the validity of this criticism, teachers focused more the next year on helping students develop critical thinking skills that they can use as they watch TV shows and read advertisements. For example, a 2nd grade teacher had her class make huge murals out of clipped magazine advertisements so students could examine what kinds of people were held up as models in our society. They found racial bias, gender stereotypes and an almost complete absence of heavy people and people with glasses. A group of teachers also used videotapes of the TV show *Mutant Ninja Turtles* and accompanying advertisements to help students examine violence on television.

Each year the site-based management council decides whether we should repeat 'no-TV week' that year and discusses possible changes in the project. We also confront difficult questions: How can we control a childhood activity that, according to the American Academy of Pediatrics, consumes more time than any other childhood activity except sleeping? How can we counter an activity that:

- fosters mental and physical passivity and undermines creativity?
- perpetuates sexual and racial stereotypes, promotes violence and encourages the buying of useless or expensive products and unhealthy food?
- presents a distorted view of reality?

How can we encourage family activities that are alternatives to TV and video game addictions, but are sensitive to the pressures of many single-parent households?

Many successes are recounted during such discussions. One parent, for example, explained that before 'no-TV week', her family always watched TV during dinner; after the week without TV, she told the children that the television would be banned during dinner so that family members could talk to each other.

Another parent decided to institute no-TV days three or four times a week. Another put the family's television in an attic room to discourage TV viewing. A fourth said her two children now ask for a no-TV night so they can play games with mum and dad.

Despite differing opinions on how best to deal with the many problems such a project engenders, the Fratney staff and

parents continue to support the effort, albeit with modifica-
tions to help enhance participation. Each year students and
adults sign no-TV contracts, keep logs of their television viewing habits, write diaries of how they survived a 'no-TV week',
interview family members about the impact of television on
their lives and examine stereotypes and advertisements on TV.

Governance

Since its inception, Fratney has been committed to governance of the school by the teachers and parents who are the
main actors at the school. This decision has not been without
conflict. For example, differences emerged over the composi-
tion of the council that would run the school. In the months
before the school opened, the steering committee of NNF was
essentially making all the decisions for the school. Power had
to be transferred from this group to the teachers who would
work there and to the parents whose children had enrolled.
One member of the steering committee suggested that the
council should include two parents elected from each of the
11 classrooms and only two teacher representatives; another
suggested that the council have equal parent and teacher representation. The matter was partially resolved when we learned
of a new agreement between the school board and the teachers'
union prescribing that all such councils need teacher representation totalling 50 per cent plus one teacher. After much
discussion, NNF decided that fighting the school board and
teachers union would be futile; instead, we decided to adhere
to the agreement, but include in our council's procedures a
provision for parent alternates that would essentially ensure
equal voice at site-based council meetings.

The site-based management council of parents and staff
members meets monthly and makes all major decisions concerning the school. We chose our principal; rewrote our report
card; developed policies regarding homework, parent involvement and multicultural education; redirected parts of our school
budget; and developed a policy that encouraged critical discussion of current events such as, at that time, the Persian Gulf

War. We also have a curriculum committee, a fund-raising committee and a building committee, the latter being a group of staff that meets regularly to deal with immediate school issues. For example, the building committee has dealt with how to provide schoolwide support for struggling new teachers and how to reapportion assignments for educational assistants among classrooms when one assistant is out for a long-term illness.

Significant parent involvement

Significant parent involvement is part of almost every successful school. Many parents were significantly involved in our struggle to establish La Escuela Fratney and develop its curriculum. Once the school opened, however, the initial euphoria diminished and parent involvement declined. The parents who remained active were mostly white and middle-class, even though white children make up a small percentage of our students.

We did three things to try to counter this imbalance and foster broader parental involvement. First, we established quotas for our site-based management council, so that African American and Latino parents were ensured seats. Second, we decided to redirect money from our budget to hire two part-time parent organizers, a Mexican American and an African American. Eventually, these two part-time positions became one full-time position. Finally, with the help of the Wisconsin Writing Project, which is part of the National Writing Project, we developed a parent project. We paid 15 parents to participate in a six-week evening workshop in which they discussed school issues and wrote about their children. Parents who did not usually participate in school activities were encouraged to participate. Several parents in the workshop have decided to remain active in other aspects of our school.

Tension between parents was sometimes a problem. For instance, middle-class white parents clashed with single mothers of African American or Latino heritage. As Christine Bowditch (1993) points out, 'The rhetoric of parent involvement, at least in many of its manifestations, assumes, legitimates, and seeks to enforce a particular normative model of the family – a model . . . that has become decreasingly representative of American families across socioeconomic classes.' At Fratney, this problem sometimes could be seen in the tendency of some middle-class parents to judge a parent's commitment to the school by the number of meetings the parent was willing to attend. These parents became 'meeting happy', wanting to schedule frequent meetings at which they work long hours. The logistics and expense of child care were not even an issue in their lives.

We have sought to overcome this problem by ensuring that meeting agendas are well planned, meetings are well run and much of the actual work is done in smaller subcommittees at times and places convenient to the parents. For example, in conjunction with a neighbourhood-based community group, our site-based council has launched a new parent group called the Friends of Fratney. The group meets monthly for breakfast immediately after the school day begins, a time that is convenient for many single mothers who drop off their children (as long as other siblings are welcome to attend).

Links to community

La Escuela Fratney is committed to community involvement because we realize that the lives of staff, students and parents extend beyond the school, and that the broader community in turn directly affects our students.

In our third year, for instance, we worked with community activists to get a new playground for young children at our school. Our 'tot lot' was dominated by a jungle gym in the shape of a tank. When we took over the school, we refused to follow the easy route to have it removed, as some in the peace movement recommended. Instead, we involved parents and students in the process and set our goal in the larger context of peace education.

Our preparation paid off when we requested that the city give us $70,000 to get a new tot lot. The mayor's office initially opposed our request, saying the city replaced only two tot lots a year and we were number 60 on the list. The thought of waiting 30 years did not hold much appeal for us. Their second argument was that if they gave into the Fratney parents and students, then other school communities would demand the same. That is exactly what should happen, we said, as we proceeded with our organizing and won the new tot lot.

Another community project involved the closing of a tavern across the street from our playground. The littering of school property and the tavern's overall negative influence on the neighbourhood convinced the site-based management council, other parents and teachers to lobby and get the tavern's liquor license revoked.

The school is currently working with local community-based organizations to plan a programme and secure funding to expand our after-school programme to better serve our students and the neighbourhood children who attend other schools.

What have we learned?

Annual budget battles have taken a toll on the Fratney project. During the last two months of each school year, we had hoped to be able to reflect on our progress and devise improvements for the following year. Instead, for three consecutive years staff and parents spent hundred of hours in communitywide efforts to prevent budget cutbacks that would have qualitatively damaged our programme. Although we have so far been successful in holding off fatal cutbacks, the energies and time expended in these efforts have significantly stalled our efforts to improve Fratney's programme.

Our commitment to site-based management has led many teachers and parents to sometimes feel swallowed up by the life of the school. Naturally, the running of the school is our top priority, but we have also felt the need to be involved in changing policies at the district level that would directly improve conditions at Fratney. Many teachers, for instance, not only fulfil their classroom duties, but also participate in the work of textbook adoption committees (Peterson 1989); city-wide teacher councils that deal with whole language instruction and multicultural curriculum; the district library council; and various task forces and commissions, especially those concerning districtwide curriculum reform (Levine 1991).

Many of the expectations we had at the beginning of this project have been turned on their head. Few people thought that approval of this neighbourhood school was a real possibility; even fewer imagined the magnitude of realizing our vision, should the proposal be approved. The process of bringing La Escuela Fratney into being has been a difficult but rewarding one that has taught us many lessons.

Lesson 1: Grass-roots movements can produce real change

An important lesson from the initial stage of our struggle is best summed up in the words of Margaret Mead: 'Never doubt that a small group of thoughtful committed citizens can change the world; indeed it's the only thing that ever has.' Both the progressive political community and the educational community in Milwaukee were shocked at our initial victory. People have become so accustomed to losing social struggles that a clear victory was unexpected. When people asked, 'How did you do it?' the simple response was 'Hard work, being well organized, and acting quickly when opportunities presented themselves.' Teachers and parents, having been inculcated during their own years of schooling with notions that the rich and famous are the makers of history, have rarely understood the importance and power of organized grass-roots movements in changing society. The power of the grass-roots movement should be an important theme woven through all school curricula.

Although a small group of individuals won the initial victory that established Fratney, it was a decision by the school board to hire more enlightened superintendents that allowed us to shift our focus from battling central office to dealing with more central educational issues. These superintendents not only supported reform, but recognized that it can be achieved only by fostering grass-roots involvement.

School reform needs small groups of committed individuals at both the district leadership levels and the building and community levels. If only the former exists, school reform fails because it has a top-down, authoritarian style that alienates the teachers who must ultimately embrace the changes that need to take place in the classroom. If support from district leadership is lacking, however, the obstacles to reform are usually so great that grass-roots activists are consumed by senseless battles diverting attention from what really needs to be done.

Lesson 2: Multiracial unity is essential to successful school reform

Another lesson from our experience is that multiracial unity is needed to move school reform forward. The initial organizing effort would have failed if African Americans, Latinos and whites had not worked closely together. Working in multiracial groups in a racially divided society is difficult; however, the success of such efforts often depends on the underlying politics of the project and the individuals involved.

In considering issues of equality and multiculturalism, people must address the issues of power and voice straight on. Who is actually in control? Whose voice is actually being heard? At Fratney, we began by deciding that antiracism and the equality of all people would be values that are taught at all grade levels. Some people of colour saw this action as a clear indication that the project was serious about building multiracial unity. We also set up decision-making groups that make parents and teachers partners in running the school. Finally, we tried to institutionalize power relationships between language-majority and language-minority students by making the two languages in question as equal as possible.

Lesson 3: Build in time to reflect and learn

A successful school programme usually cannot be planned in a hurry. Educators and parents must be willing and able to devote sufficient time to planning the programme and, later, to assessing progress and governing the school. We were able to gain additional time for teachers by (1) shifting the afternoon recess to follow lunch recess, thus extending the lunchtime planning period; (2) arranging art, music and physical education classes so that teams of teachers have time together; and (3) starting school 10 minutes earlier, so that once a month children leave early and the staff have a half day for planning.

While it is difficult finding time for staff to plan, getting time for parents and teachers to work together is even more problematic. We have found no easy solution, but have managed by making sure that our site-based council meetings are held regularly and run efficiently, so that maximum benefits come from them.

As the school has grown, the issue of time has emerged as a key problem: time to train new staff, to plan the new curriculum, to develop and implement better forms of assessment, to learn from one another. If school districts expect new and veteran teachers to improve their practices and cope with increasingly difficult social situations, qualitatively more time for collaborative planning, staff development and reflection will need to be structured into the school day and school year.

Lesson 4: Genuine parent involvement is critical

Parent involvement needs to be substantive and far-reaching. It must extend beyond fund-raisers and volunteering for field trips. The central issues are power, presence and resources. Do parents exert real power during their time spent in the school? Do parents have an ongoing, daily presence in the school and the classrooms? Are the resources allocated to schools sufficient to organize parent involvement? The Fratney experience shows that parents are more likely to come to the school if they are able to exercise genuine power in decisions that directly affect the future of the school and their children's lives. At Fratney, this has meant having parents and teachers deal with issues such as curriculum, budget, facility renovation and personnel (Peterson 1993).

Empowering parents may at times seem to work against the principles of a democratic school because some parents' ideas are neither progressive nor democratic. Parents across the United States of America, for instance, have supported book banning, lobbied for school prayer, and opposed equality and desegregation, the teaching of evolution and multiculturalism (Karp 1993).

How does a school deal with this contradiction between the need to empower parents and at the same time promote progressive educational and social policies? First, structures must be created to engender ongoing debate and constant dialogue, and these structures must not privilege those people with college education or more time. Discussion must not shy away from frank assessments of the programme's goals, expected results and alternative strategies for reaching the goals if recommended practices prove insufficient. Second, a group of people within the school must take on the task of promoting progressive policies and challenging others on such issues.

Lesson 5: Structures that foster change must be institutionalized

Although the renaissance of any particular school must be defended, we must acknowledge the limitations of school-by-school reform. Most of the fine alternative schools of the 1960s died as their originators moved on. The success of many of these schools, Fratney included, is a result of many people spending enormous amounts of time and energy in a fight against the status quo. These kinds of efforts do not readily transfer from school to school. We must institutionalize structures that allow and foster change in the public schools and in the teaching profession. For instance, paid parent organizers, based at the school level, would substantively strengthen parent involvement. Assessment procedures that are not dependent on standardized achievement tests should be adopted at district, state and national levels (that is, for Chapter I programming) to push teachers towards more holistic assessment measures.[3] Changes in state regulations governing the school calendar and hours should be made more flexible so that schools can provide more time for collaboration and planning. Districtwide programmes to support new and struggling veteran teachers should be created so that individual schools are not forced to spend inordinate amounts of time or resources on such programmes.

Lesson 6: Successful school reform is part of larger societal change efforts

On a small scale, we have seen some success with the Fratney project. Parents, staff and students continue to work together, albeit with occasional disagreement, to build a more humane, democratic school within our troubled society. The Fratney experience has shown us that the reform of any particular school must take place within a larger context of districtwide curricular reform and structural change. The improvement of schools generally must be linked to changes in society. Large class sizes, lack of teacher planning time and the broader problems of poverty, child abuse and unemployment all reflect the triumph of private profit over human need.

How can a school community work in the context of the broader struggles to make a city, state or nation a safer, healthier place to live? Our successful organizing campaign to rebuild our school 'tot lot' was a small example of a how a neighbourhood coalition can obtain funds for a project that benefits both the school and the neighbourhood. Small efforts like this can be the foundations for the development of communitywide coalitions and projects to link the generic parent at a generic school to activities and movements that will improve schools and communities alike.

Ultimately, the success of Fratney and other similar school projects is bound up tightly to our efforts to achieve justice and equality in our society as a whole. For our efforts to bear fruit, we must have both a local vision and a national vision. Just as the consciousness of my 5th grade students was in many ways linked to the march on Washington for gay and lesbian rights, so too is the future of schools like Fratney linked to broader social movements. Our schools, our cities and our children will not survive the rising tide of poverty, inequality and violence without a social movement that demands from the whole of society what many are demanding from schools alone.

Notes

1 In the 1980s, Madeline Hunter, a widely known educator, advocated for the development of lesson plans based upon seven components such as clearly stated objectives, guided practice for skill development, verbal reinforcement and active participation in learning discussions. In some schools throughout the USA, these components were taken as *the only* way to teach and were used to define effective teaching and to evaluate teacher performance in very controversial ways.
2 Chapter I is a federal programme that provides extra funding to improve the basic skills of 'disadvantaged' children.
3 While Chapter I funds may be used for a variety of initiatives, evaluation of all such funded programmes is based on pupil scores on standardized, quantitative tests of basic skills.

References

Ahlgren, P. (1993) La Escuela Fratney: Reflections on a bilingual, anti-bias, multicultural, elementary school. *Teaching Tolerance* 2(2): 26–31.

Banks, J. (1991) *Teaching Strategies for Ethnic Studies*. Boston: Allyn and Bacon.

Bowditch, C. (1993) Responses to Michelle Fine's [ap]parent involvement: Reflections on parents, power, and urban public schools. *Teachers College Record* 95(2): 177–81.

Edelsky, C. (1991) Not acquiring Spanish as a second language: The politics of second language acquisition, in *With Literacy and Justice For All: Rethinking The Social in Language and Education*. New York: Falmer Press.

Karp, S. (1993) Trouble over the rainbow. *Rethinking Schools* 7(3): 8–10.

Levine, D. (1991) A new path to learning. *Rethinking Schools* 6(1): 1, 21, 23.

Miner, B. (1991) Taking multicultural/anti-racist education seriously: An interview with Enid Lee. *Rethinking Schools* 6(1): 6.

Peterson, R. (1987) NCTE issues basal report card. *Rethinking Schools* 2(3): 6–7.

Peterson, R. (1988) Basal adoption controversy continues into second year: Whole language pilot projects launched. *Rethinking Schools* 3(1): 9.

Peterson, R. (1989) Don't mourn, organize: Teachers take the offensive against basals. *Theory into Practice* 28(4): 295–9.

Peterson, R. (1993) Creating a school that honors the traditions of a culturally diverse student body: La Escuela Fratney, in Gregory A. Smith (ed.) *Public Schools That Work: Creating Community.* New York: Routledge.

Tenorio, R. (1986) Surviving Scott Foresman: Confessions of a kindergarten teacher. *Rethinking Schools* 1(1): 1, 8.

Tenorio, R. (1988) Recipe for teaching reading: Hold the basal. *Rethinking Schools* 2(3): 4.

5

BARBARA L. BRODHAGEN

The situation made us special

Editors' introduction

Dissatisfied with the unjust and often meaningless education offered to so many youth, and unable to effect change at a whole school level, some teachers – alone or with their teaching partners – find ways to bring democratic principles to life within their own class-rooms. In this chapter, Barbara Brodhagen, a middle school (11–14-year-olds) teacher in Madison, Wisconsin, describes how she and her teaching partner created a democratic learning community in which the curriculum was collaboratively planned by students and teachers based on questions they had about themselves and the world. With that curriculum as a centre-piece, the group employed other progressive methods such as collaborative governance, co-operative learning and student-led parent conferences. All this was accomplished in the face of mandatory standardized testing and central curriculum guidelines. Successful as this effort was, it also involved difficulties – over role definitions, the constant work of finding non-textbook resources, criticism from some colleagues and other obstacles that democratic teachers have historically experienced.

We sign our constitution

The 7th grade classroom was alive with excitement and anticipation, students stretching their necks to try to look out the doorway. 'Here he comes', somebody said. Students quickly composed themselves, and all eyes were on the principal as he entered the room. Acting as spokesperson for the class, one student said, 'Mr Principal, you have been asked here today to witness the reading and signing of our classroom constitution.' One voice began as 55 others joined in:

> *We, the class of Rooms 201/202 at Marquette Middle School, in order to form the best class possible, pledge to live by the following statements:*

> - *We appreciate our individual differences. We recognize that each person is unique.*
> - *All individuals will be treated with respect and dignity. There is no room for put-downs in our room.*
> - *We will be honest with one another in order to build trust.*
> - *We will learn to resolve conflicts, which may involve learning to live with non-resolution.*
> - *Each person will truly listen to every other person.*
> - *We will cooperate and collaborate with one another.*
> - *Learning will be meaningful.*
> - *We recognize that people learn in different ways.*

> *Assignments, field trips, hands-on experiences will be varied so that everyone can and will learn. If everyone tries, we ALL will succeed.*

> - *Having fun will naturally become part of our experiences.*
> - *All individuals will be organized and on time.*
> - *We will respect the right to pass (not take a turn).*

> *We agree to abide by these truths to the best of our abilities, both as unique individuals and as a cooperative and collaborative community.*

One young person began to clap, and soon there were cheers and more applause for all of us, and each of us, and what we had done.

The principal said some appropriate and encouraging words and left. We were a group of people, young adolescents and adults, who had just publicly stated agreement to all that was in our constitution, and each of us would try to honour its content to the best of our ability.

Few teachers would be willing to step into a classroom and attempt to engage more than four dozen 12- and 13-year-olds in meaningful discussion. We have all read about how unruly large groups of young adolescents can be, and many of us are afraid we would be unable to 'keep control' in this setting. But if creating a democratic community is our goal, then every young person must have a chance to be heard and teachers must be willing to listen. Achieving such a community is what this chapter is about. It is the story of how teachers and students at Marquette Middle School (now known as Georgia O'Keefe Middle School) in Madison, Wisconsin, worked together to create a democratic classroom.

Marquette Middle School has a culturally diverse enrolment of about 600 students, many of whom are eligible for free or reduced-price lunches. Classes are heterogeneously grouped, and students who need special education are integrated into all classes. School administrators have supported new teaching innovations.

During the two years from which this story is told, as many as 56 heterogeneously grouped students were assigned to two teachers who had responsibility for maths/science and language arts/social studies. They were joined by a special education teacher who had been assigned to work with students who were 'learning disabled'. Each semester, a student teacher from the university worked with us as well.

What brought me to this

I have been teaching for a long time. For many years, I worked with children identified as having a learning disability. This work gave me the unique opportunity to get into many classrooms in several school districts in Wisconsin and New York.

Rarely did I see students in any of those classrooms participate in determining what they were to learn or how they would learn it.

Much of what happened in those classrooms did not seem to make sense to students, and teachers rarely tried to connect what students were learning from one class to the next. Students' usual routine was to sit and listen for 45 minutes and then go to the next class and do the same. When young people asked, 'Why do we have to learn this?' or 'Is this going to be on the test?' or 'Do we have to remember this?', I was sometimes not really sure how to answer them. The students, both learning-disabled and not, were frustrated, and so was I.

As a result of these less-than-satisfying experiences as a teacher (as well as some during my own student years), I began talking to colleagues and friends, trying to create another view of school. We talked of designing school experiences that involve students in all aspects of classroom life, including curriculum planning. Curriculum integration, an idea I had almost forgotten, seemed to provide the theoretical framework needed for this endeavour. I recalled my earlier teaching experiences in a self-contained, integrated middle school classroom for the learning-disabled. In that classroom, students planned their learning with me. They taught their hobbies and interests to one another. Those times had slipped away from me.

Integrative curriculum, planning with students, cooperative learning, team teaching – all were part of what I knew would help bring about successful teaching and learning experiences for teachers and students, including students labelled learning-disabled. I explained to our building administrators what I wanted to do, then set out to find someone who would team with me. Mary Ploeser, a maths and science teacher, happily accepted my invitation. I was excited to start the school year.

We create a community

Teachers did not walk into the classroom on the first day of school and ask students to write a classroom constitution.

We and our students were strangers, representing different neighbourhoods, socioeconomic levels and ethnic backgrounds. The first two days of the school year were filled with the busy work common to most schools: locker assignments, class schedules, school forms, and so on. We had, however, planned some introductory activities. Half-way through the second day, we asked students how they thought all of us might get to know one another and create a real community. This simple question was the first of many invitations for young people to help create a democratic community. Students did not hesitate; ideas poured forth.

The theme for the first two weeks was 'Who are we? Who am I?', a theme selected by the teachers. Students and teachers together decided that a survey to which everyone contributed questions would help us find out more about one another.

The group wanted to know where everyone had come from, so we designed a family history form, and each person went home and recorded all the countries their ancestors had come from. The information from the forms was used to make maps identifying these countries and to compute each country's distance from Madison. Students investigated whether the countries' names had changed by comparing old world maps to new world maps. These young adolescents, each trying to find his or her own identity, wanted to know what their names meant, so off they went to the library to research both first and last names. Teachers did these same activities. After all, we were members of the group too.

To help answer the question 'Who am I?', we measured heights, gathered family health and education histories, wrote brief autobiographies (complete with snapshots) and compared individual data to the results of the class survey. We all marked the location of our homes on a local map. Students interviewed one another and made introductions to the entire group.

Students suggested there be rules for the class, both for teachers and for students. If there were to be rules, then those who would have to live by the rules needed to have a say. The group discussed whether these 'things' should be called rules, guidelines, or a contract. One student suggested we write a constitution. Teachers led a review on constitutions and students and teachers made separate lists of ideas that might be included in a class constitution. Both lists were displayed, and teachers and students debated and negotiated whether various requests were legitimate and, if they were, whether they belonged in our constitution. Teachers and students alike had to stand up and explain, provide evidence, or otherwise convince the group why a particular idea or statement was necessary. After reaching consensus, a committee of students and one teacher took the short phrases, ideas and complete sentences and fashioned them into the previously quoted constitution.

The constitution guided us throughout the school year. On numerous occasions, students, more than teachers, called the group's attention to statements made and agreed upon. It was clear they did not take the group's efforts lightly.

Other activities helped build community throughout the year. All of us participated in cooperative games, went to the school forest ropes course, had a potluck dinner, invited parents to see projects and hear presentations, shared our successes with other classes and invited support staff to be part of the activities.

Another idea that initially met with sniggers, but ended up being a favourite, was Monday morning 'sharing time'. Any student or students could share something they had done, something that had happened, or something they had heard about. On most Mondays, a time limit was necessary because so many students wanted to participate. We heard about many wonderful experiences and also about the many stresses some of these young people lived under. 'Sharing time' gave all of us a chance to get to know different sides of people, what they did in their free time, what their family was like, and what they heard on the news. We valued this time and considered it an important part of our democratic community.

From this partial description of the first two weeks of school, you can see that students already had many opportunities to participate in the creation of a community. We listened to all ideas, and by doing so, honoured the diversity represented in the classroom: female and male, rich and poor, adult and young adolescent and people of many ethnic groups.

Our survey had shown us that we did not agree on everything, but had decided that certain things were important to
us all. We shared a sense of who we were and we had begun to
trust one another. We were becoming a community.

We plan together

The constitution written jointly by teachers and students stated
that 'learning will be meaningful'. One way we try to assure meaningful learning is to involve students in planning the curriculum.

The purpose of our curriculum is to help young people extend their understanding of themselves and their world. Using
a constructivist approach, we ask students to identify questions
and concerns they have about self and the world.

Here are some of students' questions about self:

How did my skin colour come about? What will happen to
me after I die? Why was I born who I am and into my family?
Will my kids follow in my footsteps? Why is school so hard
for me? How do my bodily organs keep going and going? How
will I know if I am really in love? Will I be successful and
happy? Why am I so short?

And here are some of students' questions about the world:

Why do some people/groups think they are better? How did
racism ever start? How did religions evolve? Is it possible for
people to be born with both sex parts? Why are some people
gay? When will gang violence ever stop? Why are so many
politicians dishonest? Will there ever be a President who is not
a white man? Will there ever be enough for all to survive?
What would happen if the sun died? How was the universe
created? How can birds fly? Will other planets be inhabitable?
Will the earth become so crowded that some will be sent to
space? What will people evolve to look like in a hundred
years? Will there ever be a cure for AIDS? Why can't teenagers
vote? How do roller coasters work? Why are some kids popular? Why do we only hear about the bad stuff?

Students first develop their questions individually and then
work in small groups to try to find common or shared questions.
Once the whole class has identified these questions, students

are asked to find connections between the self and world questions. These connections form themes around which the curriculum is organized. Students have developed such themes as the Future; 'Isms'; Outer Space; Time: Past and Present; Mind Bogglers; Environment; Death, War, and Violence; and Conflict.

As students consider each theme, they identify activities that respond to the self and world questions included in the theme. A curriculum containing activities suggested by students begins to accommodate individual learning styles, what a person likes to do or is good at. Students know that they need to develop a variety of skills, however. When asked what should happen if the only suggested activity was 'to read', students were quick to respond that there has to be a balance; everyone needs to do the basics, 'like reading, writing, and maths, and all that other stuff we learn in school'.

The teacher's role in this process is not the traditional one of always directing the action from the front of the classroom, but rather one of facilitating activities and collaborating with students. We help groups of students hold discussions, model how to ask clarifying questions, suggest ways to phrase questions, listen to be sure that one or two students do not control a group, and offer encouragement and suggestions. We help students hear others' ideas and periodically remind them that each person has a right to an opinion.

Many wonderful things can happen when students and teachers jointly plan the curriculum. Everyone has opportunities to participate in making decisions about what our work will be. Young people see their teachers listening to them and treating them seriously. Respect and trust between students and teachers grow as both observe how actions and words bring the curriculum to life. The early group planning we did created a climate of openness for the rest of the year, a large part of which was a curriculum with far fewer 'hidden' aspects than a traditional curriculum.

We have big questions and concerns

It would take many pages to list all the questions students have raised in our classroom. The self and world questions mentioned earlier should be enough to convince anyone that young people have limitless questions and concerns about themselves and the world. They are curious about almost everything and are trying hard to make sense of life in all its complexities, and to find out who they are and what they want to become. Their serious and thoughtful questions reflect a need to see themselves as members of a variety of groups within numerous cultures, including the dominant culture.

In the search to find answers, the group often went in directions not planned. One question usually led to several new questions, usually along the lines of '*Why does it have to be that way?*' or '*Who says so?*' or '*Who makes the decisions?*' or '*Why don't we just change it?*' Because democracy, dignity and diversity were at the centre of our classroom, we tried to look at each question and theme through these lenses. If students did not bring up these questions, teachers did. We wanted students to become accustomed to looking at what they studied with a critical eye and to considering as many different viewpoints as possible.

For example, an activity in the 'Isms' unit was designed to answer several questions about the relative anonymity of women who have invented things or spearheaded important social movements. Students studied women who have made notable contributions towards the improvement of humankind and then tried to locate information about these women in a huge stack of the school's social studies and history textbooks. Students were surprised to find little mention of the women in the textbooks and immediately wanted to know why they had been left out of these chronicles of history.

We talked about who writes textbooks, who owns textbook companies, how society has treated the contributions of women throughout history and what people could do to hear the complete story. Students were reminded of other work done during the year that also highlighted the prevalent practice of omitting specific groups of people. Students learned that they can use textbooks to answer some questions, but they also learned that they need to consult a variety of sources for complete answers to other questions. Their research experiences showed them that there are sometimes discrepancies in the information presented in resources on the same topic, that 'reliable' sources are not always accurate.

Anyone who has worked in a middle school can tell you that adolescents are concerned about fairness and justice in solving the problems of society. They are thinking through their own ideas about morality and going through the sometimes painful process of deciding whether they will continue to abide by the values 'given' to them. We challenged students to think critically about their questions and encouraged them to keep asking tough questions of their teachers, their parents and even their peers. The depth of young adolescents' questions is surprising even to teachers who work with them every day. We sometimes wonder whether we thought about these 'big' questions when we were their age; we know that nobody ever encouraged us to.

When we asked parents to identify their own questions and concerns about themselves and the world as part of an 'open house' presentation, they came up with many of the same questions that their children did:

- Where are the dirtiest and cleanest cities? cultures?
- Why are there not more recycled products?
- Why do we kill so many animals for food?
- How can we create and save jobs and save the animals and the environment?
- What is the status of the space station?
- How much do we spend on outer space?
- Who owns outer space?
- Will racism ever stop?
- Why do people kill each other (not in war)?
- Will there ever be a time when everyone has enough to survive?
- What job will I have? What kind of jobs will there be?
- Will we keep growing in number until we are wiped out?
- Will children our age ever be able to vote?

We believe students have the right to try to figure out how things got to be the way they are. There have been times, however, when we have stared at the long lists of questions and activities suggested by students and wondered how we would ever find the strength to teach about some of these over-whelming, real life issues. During those moments, we remind ourselves of students' intense desire *to know why things are*, and then reaffirm our commitment to helping these children find the answers.

I know that what happened in our classroom is not common. In many classrooms, questions from students are unwelcome, but we continue to believe that young people have the right to ask questions and 'the right to know'. They have the right to be part of a school that deals with their questions seriously.

Students are involved in developing their own evaluations

'Welcome to the Room 201/202 Museum.'

'The museum tour is about to begin. Would you please line up behind your tour guide?' Groups of young people shuffle around, some find seats, others gather papers, and a small group lines up in the front of the room.

'My name is Lisa and I will be your first guide. I will explain to you what a rain forest is and where rain forests are located. Other guides will show and tell you about the products, climate, rainfall, groundwater, soil conditions, and endangered plants and animals of rain forests. You will also hear about indigenous peoples and reasons why the rain forests are in the news. And you will find out some strange but true facts about rain forests.'

Looking around the room, visitors see more than a rain forest. A child's plastic swimming pool has been turned into a pond complete with water, grass, tadpoles, and a frog. There is a woodland forest made of branches covered with a variety of leaves and all sorts of stuffed animals: deer, raccoon, birds, and bear. A papier-mache snake slithers in desert sand as a vulture flies overhead. Visitors see groundwater displays, charts, posters, dioramas, and 'Do you know?' displays. The room is alive with color.

At various points in the museum, student tour guides discuss different topics. At the front of the room, Jeff is describing the rain

*forest food chain. He holds up pictures of a poisonous tree frog and
a leaf on which there are tiny insects. Then he replaces the picture
of the frog with a picture of a toucan and begins to talk about
animals and plants on the endangered species list.*

*At the close of the tour, the rain forest guides ask for questions.
Many hands shoot into the air. The guides answer those questions
they can and write down those they can't, assuring the group that
the museum staff will 'get right on it' and find the answers. They
thank the group for coming and return to their seats as the next
biome's guides move into place.*

Much had to happen before museum tours like this could
take place. First, students had to decide what biome they wanted
to study. Then the large group, including the teachers, had to
determine the requirements to be met by each small group.
Group members had to decide who was going to do what
research. Research had to be completed before any construction could begin. Decisions had to be made about where biomes
would be built. Maps needed to be drawn, reports written,
speeches practised and on and on. The guided museum tour
was each group's final evaluation for the 'Environment' unit.
The tour was videotaped by a teacher, the list of requirements
checked by the teachers and the tour evaluated by students.

Students often were involved in creating unit or theme evaluations, which might be a final group project, a presentation, or
a written self-evaluation. For instance, students developed a
multimedia presentation to teach a different age group about
an 'ism'; made a collage, book, or box to show what they
thought life would be like in the future; completed individual
and group requirements for a presentation about a planet in
our solar system; and did community service as a part of the
'Environment' unit. Teachers were willing to listen and negotiate with students when they presented their ideas about how
evaluation might occur, sending students the message that
their ideas mattered.

Students completed self-evaluations at the end of themes and
marking periods. Teachers and students spent time discussing
areas that the evaluation might include, such as quality and

quantity of work, what was easy and hard, students' effort and interest, what they liked to do best or least, group versus individual work skills, and so on. After reviewing their 'portfolio' of completed work, students wrote about what they thought they had learned. Finally, students wrote goals for the next marking period.

We cannot believe how much we have learned

Every 'product' or paper copy of each student's work was collected and kept to provide students with a visible record of their work. This 'portfolio' served as the basis for students' written self-evaluations. As students went through their papers, we heard time and time again, 'I can't believe we did so much work.'

Every student had a notebook to use as an individual processing journal. Near the end of each day, teachers put questions on the board that called for students to reflect on critical learnings or 'big' concepts. The written responses to these questions allowed teachers to check in with every student and get feedback about our teaching. When many students could not answer the questions, we knew we had to provide additional learning experiences.

Teachers met with groups of 8–10 students to discuss the current theme and to consider students' concerns, reactions to activities, or requests for additional teaching or practice. Teachers used this time to bring up critical learnings that students should be mastering, to ask students to explain what they have been doing and to ask for feedback about a variety of things.

At the end of each theme, teachers and students attempted to list the knowledge and skills students had needed to answer their questions. We realized that this 'new' curriculum approach would prompt someone to ask for documentation of students' learning. What better way for us to gather this information than by asking the group? By middle school, most students are able to use the language of education, so they listed, for example, 'read, write, communicate, do research, use maths, work with maps, graphs, and tables, use the scientific method, use computers, listen, give reports and work in groups'.

Listing learnings on the board, talking in small processing groups and having individuals write in a processing journal all helped us know whether students were learning. At times, the group was amazed at how much they had accomplished and learned. By answering their own questions, the young people could see a purpose in learning, for example, how to compute the mean, median and mode, or how to contact an environmental agency. They had many opportunities to see the connection between the what, how and why of learning because they were being asked to create knowledge based on their own real work; they were being asked to actively educate themselves.

We wanted students to learn a great deal – and to know that they had. We wanted them to be able to reflect on the most recent theme or the entire year and clearly see their many accomplishments. We wanted them to understand that even though they were not studying the separate subjects of the traditional curriculum, they were learning much of what the 'education community' said they should learn.

Everyone works together

Students worked with one another much of the time. Often we had each student name one person with whom she or he felt able to work; then teachers structured heterogeneous cooperative learning groups. The groups stayed constant throughout an activity and sometimes throughout an entire theme. We tried to change the make-up of groups across the year, however, so that students had opportunities to work with all of their classmates. The strategy must have worked, because our students have told us that in other classes they knew only a few of their classmates, but in our classroom they know everyone.

Our constitution called for collaboration and cooperation. We wanted to eliminate as much competition as possible. The students who had the most difficulty adjusting to a lack of obvious competition were the high-achieving students. Because they were not completing many worksheets or individual assignments, but instead were doing individual and group projects, they initially were unsure they were still doing well. After several weeks, however, these students began to see that cooperating with others did not compromise their own academic work. They also realized that the projects and other activities in our curriculum were more challenging and sophisticated than the worksheets they were used to completing.

Students began to see that they could be teachers to each other and did not depend as much on the 'official' teachers. After all, the teachers were often trying to answer questions along with the students. By learning together, we were experiencing the creation of knowledge based on our questions. We worked together toward a common goal important to us all, and when a unit was finished, we applauded and cheered in celebration of all completed projects and presentations.

Do you want to talk to our class?

We frequently invited people from the community to our class to help us try to answer the questions students had raised. Students were always suggesting, 'Bring in an expert'. It was astounding how many human resources students helped us locate. They knew all sorts of people, and those we called were glad to help out, especially if we mentioned the name of the student who had made the recommendation. Our presenters were usually surprised at how specific our requests for information were, and many commented on how well prepared the class was for their visit. Some were also surprised at the topics being studied.

We wanted to open students' minds to many career possibilities, so our presenters were almost always asked to talk about the education needed for their present occupation. White-collar professionals, tradespeople, service providers, retired workers, people working in jobs out of the mainstream, and even an AIDS care provider came to speak to us. Our class learned from these people, and they learned from us.

Students join the parent-teacher conferences

Everything was set. All the student work portfolios were in order, the room was relatively pleasant, the table and chairs were in position, and I was nervous. 'Will this really work?' I wondered. 'Will these kids really conduct their own parent-student-teacher conferences? Had there been enough preparation? Will parents want to listen to their child?'

I glanced at the clock and knew it was time. My first conference was with Holly, a bright young adolescent who does consistently good work, but doesn't seem to want to participate in large- or small-group discussions.

Holly walked into the room first and came right to the table and sat down. Trailing behind was her mother, who was carrying a younger sibling. I slid Holly's folder toward her, waiting for her to make introductions. 'And who is this?' I asked, as I leaned over and touched the sibling's hand. With that, Holly began.

She introduced her mother, her sister, and me and then plunged into discussion of her work. 'This is my best work.' She took papers out and gave a brief explanation of each. Her mom asked questions and made comments such as 'I remember when you were working on this' and 'This turned out pretty good.' Holly explained that the 'best' papers would be kept at school in a folder that would be sent home at year's end, with all the other 'best' papers.

Holly then read her written self-evaluation to her mom. When she had finished, she and her mom started to talk about why Holly didn't want to talk in front of her peers. Her mom admitted that as a teenager she didn't want to talk in class either. They talked about what was easy and challenging for Holly. They laughed about Holly's admission that doing her homework in front of the television wasn't such a good idea. And they discussed her goals for the next quarter, with mom saying Holly was too hard on herself.

I just sat there, amazed. Holly had said all I would have said, and much more that I never could or should. I simply validated a lot of what they had said. When it was over, the three of us stood, smiling at one another, exchanging looks that seemed to say, 'This felt good, let's do it again.'

The parent-teacher conferences held in previous years were always somewhat disappointing for us. Students, the critical focus of the conference, usually were not even present. We decided to begin our overhaul of the conferences by asking students how they thought the conferences should be structured. They were quick to point out that the parents or other concerned adults who attended these conferences heard the same things year after year: 'Dan could do better if he only would pay attention.' 'Brian should participate more in class.' 'Jamie is doing just fine.' 'Ali doesn't complete her assignments.' 'Tim talks with his friends too much during class.' Students said their parents would come home from the conference and ground them if they had done poorly or hardly talk about the conference at all if it had gone well. They asked if it wouldn't be more beneficial to talk about their good points, since both the student and parent generally already knew what the student should do better.

Together we decided that conferences would focus on what students defined as their 'best work' and also include a review of students' written self-evaluations and goals. 'Best work' was a collection of five or six pieces that students selected using their own criteria. These might have included a favourite, one that received a good grade, one that was of interest, or one that looked hard; some students chose papers that represented a cross-section of work in writing, maths, social studies, or other areas. The remainder of students' work was available for review and would be sent home at the conclusion of the conference.

As you can see from the example above, what really sets these conferences apart is that students direct the action, from making necessary introductions and beginning the conference, to wrapping up the discussion at the appropriate time. Students can begin the conference with a discussion of any of the three sections of the conference folder: (1) the written self-evaluation, (2) the official school report card, or (3) the 'best work'. At some point in the discussion, however, they must describe what they have been studying and show the related work, highlighting their 'best' work. During most conferences, parents ask clarifying questions that prompt students to offer additional information. The written self-evaluation can be read aloud by the student or given to the parent to read. Goals, too, must be discussed.

The teacher enters into the conversation only as needed. We have found that students are quite capable of assessing their strengths and weaknesses; in many cases, we have even had to soften their too-harsh self-evaluations.

For many of these young people and their parents, the conferences are one of the few times they actually discuss the 'work' of the student. Most students can point out what they are good at and what they still need to work on. All the 'old' conference items come out through the self-evaluation and goals, but this conference format gives students a large measure of control over what and how things are said. Shifting who has the 'power' in various situations is an important part of creating a democratic classroom.

We look back on our experiences

It is now two years since I began working with and in an integrative curriculum where student-teacher planning is a given. I can no longer imagine not involving the learners, no matter their age, in planning their education and running 'our' classroom. Each school year, students have clearly demonstrated that they are able and willing to actively participate in planning and designing their own education.

Some students initially said the work of planning the curriculum was too difficult and asked, 'Why don't you teachers just do all of it?' We were asking them to become learners who actively participate in all aspects of their education, from planning to evaluation, and most had never been asked to do anything like that before. They were uncomfortable with changing the role of students. The role of teachers changed too. Sometimes teachers were still disseminators of information, but more often we were learners as well as facilitators of learning.

Teachers and students struggled to define and act on these new roles. Deciding when students would participate in decisions and when teachers alone would make decisions was a recurring issue. Students sometimes challenged teachers to explain why students could not be part of all decisions. Many times, we had no answer for them. We were still trying to figure out how much 'control' could or should be given to students. All of us were learning firsthand how difficult it can be to put democratic principles into action.

Student-teacher planning of the curriculum was a messy process. We did not have a neat curriculum guide or textbook to turn to for lessons. Identifying the significant concepts that would tie a theme together took a lot of time, but without this identification, a theme could become a series of 'sound bites' that did little to satisfy students' need to learn. There were many times when teachers had to scramble to find appropriate materials and resources. Fortunately, we had the much-needed planning time to accomplish these tasks.

Colleagues' reactions to our efforts varied greatly. Some thought we were just going into class and doing whatever the students wanted to do. Some wondered if we were teaching anything. Some knew and understood what we were doing, but said they would never try it because they could see how much extra work it requires. Very few asked to talk with us about our work, yet we knew some were talking about it without us being present to explain. The administration did not put up any roadblocks, but nobody made any overt efforts to invite others to critically consider the nature and substance of our work.

At the time I became involved in this effort, I did not think about it as trying to create a democratic classroom. I wanted the students to work with teachers in creating an exciting, rich and meaningful curriculum. I wanted to see and hear for myself that young people can learn and want to learn. I did not know how the effort would turn out, and I still have many questions, but they concern implementation rather than theory. As I have said, I cannot go back.

The teachers involved in this endeavour interviewed former students to learn what they miss the most about our classrooms. They miss having a say in what they learn, being able to study something in depth, working in groups, knowing they can bring up an issue even if it is not on the agenda, making presentations about what they learned, talking politics and participating in making decisions about much of the day-to-day life of the classroom.

As part of the interview, we asked the group if they thought the computer had perhaps generated a 'special' group rather than the diverse, heterogeneous one it was directed to. After all, our time together had been a great success in so many ways for nearly everyone involved that the experience seemed almost too good to be true. After some discussion, one student said what we all felt: '. . . We weren't a special group, but the situation made us special.'

6 | MICHAEL W. APPLE AND JAMES A. BEANE

Lessons from democratic schools

We live in a time when the very meaning of democracy is being radically changed. Rather than referring to ways in which political and institutional life are shaped by equitable, active, widespread and fully informed participation, democracy is increasingly being defined as unregulated business manœuvres in a free market economy. Applied to schools, this redefinition has given rise to the push for tax credits and vouchers, management by private firms, commercialized media and materials, and abandonment of the broader ideals of public education (Apple 1993). This degradation has extended to the point where a private consulting firm has recommended that 'public' be dropped from 'public schools' in the USA because its similar use in conjunction with housing, libraries, radio, and assistance programmes has come to have negative connotations. Such is the power of language manipulation: Social commitments for the common good are now made out to be 'public nuisances'.

The schools described in this book are part of a larger movement that eschews this redefinition of democracy in education.

They are deeply involved in finding practical ways to increase the meaningful participation of everyone involved in the educational experience, including parents, local residents and especially students themselves. From their experiences, we can see that this goal is attainable through the creation of learning communities within each school and between the school and the larger community (see also Smith 1993).

The curriculum in all of these schools is based on the belief that knowledge comes to life for students and teachers only when it is connected to something that is serious. Rigorous intellectual work is prized, not for the sake of symbolic standards or agreeable publicity, but because of its ability to make a difference in how we understand and act powerfully on the social world in which we live. The implications for a process of assessment dramatically different from the relatively mechanical and reductive standardized procedures used by so many school systems are visible in these pioneering schools as well.

The idea of a thematic curriculum dominates these schools, not simply as an effective methodology that keeps children happy, but because this approach involves putting knowledge to use in relation to real life problems and issues (Beane 1993). The focus on what is called 'unmet community needs' in Rindge, on social and environmental issues at Fratney and Marquette, or on finding answers to 'serious questions' at Central Park East is there because knowledge is thought about differently. Rather than being lists of concepts, facts and skills that students master for standardized achievement tests (and then go on to forget, by and large), knowledge is that which is intimately connected to the communities and biographies of real people. Students learn that knowledge makes a difference in people's lives, including their own.

This view of knowledge can be seen in the emphasis at Rindge on transforming vocational education. Here, vocational education is not simply teaching future workers the flexible job skills supposedly needed for the twenty-first century, for despite political and educational rhetoric to the contrary, most economic forecasts show that a large proportion of the jobs the modern economy is creating are low-skilled, part-time and poorly paid (Apple 1989). Vocational education at Rindge is designed as preparation for an enhanced model of active citizenship in which all people are empowered to make important decisions about the institutions in which they live and work – now and in the future. This same understanding can be seen in the emphasis at Marquette, Fratney, and Central Park East on developing curricula that speak to the present concerns and future dreams of the students, teachers and communities that have so much to gain and lose in these schools.

We do not want to be dewy-eyed romantics here. The authors of these chapters are honest about the challenges they still face: financial cuts, pressure from powerful groups to define school purposes in terms of business community needs, ultra-conservative attacks on programmes and materials, the obsession with measuring anything that moves in the classroom, bureaucratic intransigence and a society that has been told that public schools cannot work in creative ways. What is perhaps most impressive about these schools is their remarkable progress in the face of such challenges. There are lessons to be learned here.

One fact that emerges clearly from these accounts is the attention educators give to the 'mundane' realities of daily life in schools. These stories remind us that the most powerful meaning of democracy is formed not in glossy political rhetoric, but in the details of everyday lives. In these schools, people take seriously the realities of curriculum development, teaching, assessment and the lives of students and teachers who must cooperate to make schools actually work. To say that people are committed to such matters may seem a needless restatement of the obvious; after all, the same topics are part of almost any 'reform' talk in almost any faculty room. What is striking about these educators, however, is that they refused to allow the difficult financial stringencies we are all under, the often unwieldy bureaucratic regulations of many school systems, and the immense social pressures and demands being placed on schools to get in the way of building educational experiences that make a real difference in the lives of their students. In viewing such conditions as challenges to be dealt with, not excuses for inaction, these educators have shown a quality that more of us should aspire to, the quality of uncommon courage.

These educators have also managed to evoke an education that is both disciplined and caring; they do not provide formulas for students, teachers, or administrators. An education of this sort is the result of hard work by *everyone* involved. From our experience with the educators who have written in this book, we know such work is compelling and fulfilling, but almost always exhausting. Yet, as almost any educator knows, we are all exhausted at the end of a day spent dealing with the realities of schools. The people whose voices you have heard here, however, have made a choice: Rather than spending most of their time on administrative tasks, curricula, teaching and evaluation that are disconnected from their students and from the communities that they serve, rather than continuing to reproduce the conditions that make so many of our most talented teachers and administrators feel frustrated in their day-to-day lives, they have decided to make a break. They have decided to devote their lives as educators to engaging in educational activity organized around democratic social and pedagogic principles in which they strongly believe. In other words, they have chosen to be exhausted as a result of something worthwhile.

Our analysis to this point implies that these chapters, and their authors, describe an important break from 'traditional' practice. Well, yes and no. They do stand as articulate statements about what is possible in schools if people are willing to move away from simply echoing the rhetoric of democracy and instead take up the practical tasks involved in building more democratic schools. As we note in Chapter 1, however, these schools and classrooms have not broken away from a tradition; they have found their way back to it. One of the distinct tragedies of today's school reform efforts is that the people involved have almost no knowledge of the long and valued tradition of like-minded efforts. Unfortunately, educators and citizens alike seem to have virtually no collective memory of the many successful attempts at building more democratic schools. The history of progressive school reform documents the fact that thousands of teachers, administrators, community activists and others spent their entire professional lives trying to build more educationally and socially respons- ive institutions. We have much to gain by reconnecting with their successes and with how they approached and overcame difficulties. All progressively inclined educators stand on the shoulders of these people, people whose eloquent vision and hard work day in and day out stand as reminders that what the educators in this book are now doing in real schools is a continuation of a long and wide river of democracy. Our tasks as educators are to keep the river flowing on course and to enable all of the children of this nation to participate in this process.

We have presented four descriptions of democratic schools in this book. There are many, many more that could and probably should be shared among us. In our inner cities, in rural areas and elsewhere, dedicated educators and community members have formed coalitions to take democracy seriously. One of the very real dilemmas educators face is finding out what is going on in school systems throughout this country where progressive schooling is making an impact. Part of the problem is simply time. Our work has become so intensified (Apple 1988, 1993) that not only is it difficult to find time to write about our successes, it is sometimes difficult to find time to even read about what other people are doing to trans- form their schools. Yet sharing our stories is crucial, as is teach- ing one another what can be done, what pitfalls to avoid and what reality is like when the hard work of building more responsive schools finally pays off.

There are many places where educators can turn to tell their stories and to hear what others are doing: groups such as Re- thinking Schools in Milwaukee, the Institute for Democracy in Education in Ohio, Educators for Social Responsibility, the National Coalition of Educational Activists and publications such as *Teaching Tolerance, Rethinking Schools, Democracy and Education,* and *Equity and Excellence.* These groups and publica- tions provide forums for sharing and hearing that will do much to counter the cynicism and despair that many educators feel when confronted with the daily difficulties of doing their jobs well in these uncertain times.

We include ourselves in the group that wants to learn about what is happening in the schools, because we understand that philosophical statements can find meaning only in the light of the experiences of real schools. We encourage you to tell us about your own experience in establishing programmes similar to those described here. We may find, then, that this volume becomes only the first in a series recounting the rise of democratic schools. In this way, we can document that our best hope for countering the arrogant tendencies now being pushed on schools by groups with authoritarian political agendas, by the centralizers and by the privatizers is to demonstrate that there are state schools that *do* work, and they do so by bringing real democracy to life. Our children's lives and futures are at stake. Let us not wait for others to act.

References

Apple, Michael W. (1988) *Teachers and Texts*. New York: Routledge.

Apple, Michael W. (1989) American realities: Poverty, economy and education, in Lois Weis, Eleanor Farrar, and Hugh G. Petrie (eds) *Dropouts from School: Issues, Dilemmas, and Solutions*. Albany: State University of New York Press.

Apple, Michael W. (1993) *Official Knowledge: Democratic Education in a Conservative Age*. New York: Routledge.

Beane, James A. (1993) *A Middle School Curriculum*. Columbus, Ohio: National Middle School Association.

Smith, Gregory A. (1993) *Public Schools That Work*. New York: Routledge.